MW01170026

If found please return this

PARAGLIDING

JOURNAL

to:

_____

_____

PARAGLIDING JOURNAL

CASE OF EMERGENCY

FLYER DETAILS

OWNER NAME	
FULL ADDRESS	
EMAIL & NUMBER	
EMERGENCY CONTACT	
EMERGENCY NUMBER	
DOCTOR DETAILS	

INCIDENT DETAILS

LOCATION		DATE
PARAGLIDER		
PARAMOTOR		/ /

LAUNCH TYPE		AIRTIME	
		AIR DISTANCE	

WEATHER CONDITION	☀ ☁ ❄ ⛈ 🌬	TIME OF YEAR	🌷 ☀ 🍃 ❄

FLIGHT START	🕐	GEAR CHECKLIST	
FLIGHT FINISH		☐ PARAGLIDER	☐ HARNESS
SLOPE GRADIENT	↕	☐ GOGGLES	☐ HELMET
		☐ RESERVE	☐ GLOVES

LAUNCH LOCATION	LANDING LOCATION

NOTES & OBSERVATIONS

AIRTIME DURATION		FLIGHT CENTER STAMP	
TODAY			☐ INSTRUCTOR
TO DATE			☐ FLIGHT TUTOR
ALL TIME			☐ FLIGHT BUDDY

SIGNATURE

LOCATION		DATE
PARAGLIDER		
PARAMOTOR		/ /

LAUNCH TYPE		AIRTIME	
		AIR DISTANCE	

WEATHER CONDITION	☀ ☁ ❄ ⛈ 🌬	TIME OF YEAR	🌷 ☀ 🍂 ❄

FLIGHT START	🕐	GEAR CHECKLIST	
FLIGHT FINISH		☐ PARAGLIDER	☐ HARNESS
SLOPE GRADIENT	↕	☐ GOGGLES	☐ HELMET
		☐ RESERVE	☐ GLOVES

LAUNCH LOCATION	LANDING LOCATION

NOTES & OBSERVATIONS

_____

_____

AIRTIME DURATION		FLIGHT CENTER STAMP	
TODAY			☐ INSTRUCTOR
TO DATE			☐ FLIGHT TUTOR
ALL TIME			☐ FLIGHT BUDDY

SIGNATURE
_____

LOCATION		DATE
PARAGLIDER		
PARAMOTOR		/ /

LAUNCH TYPE		AIRTIME	
		AIR DISTANCE	

WEATHER CONDITION	☀ ☁ ❄ ⛈ 🌬	TIME OF YEAR	🌷 ☀ 🍃 ❄

FLIGHT START	🕐	GEAR CHECKLIST	
FLIGHT FINISH		☐ PARAGLIDER	☐ HARNESS
SLOPE GRADIENT	↕	☐ GOGGLES	☐ HELMET
		☐ RESERVE	☐ GLOVES

LAUNCH LOCATION	LANDING LOCATION

NOTES & OBSERVATIONS

_____

_____

_____

AIRTIME DURATION		FLIGHT CENTER STAMP
TODAY		☐ INSTRUCTOR
TO DATE		☐ FLIGHT TUTOR
ALL TIME		☐ FLIGHT BUDDY

SIGNATURE _____

LOCATION		DATE
PARAGLIDER		
PARAMOTOR		/ /

LAUNCH TYPE		AIRTIME	
		AIR DISTANCE	

WEATHER CONDITION	☀ ☁ ❄ ⛈ 💨	TIME OF YEAR	🌷 ☀ 🍁 ❄

FLIGHT START	🕐	GEAR CHECKLIST	
FLIGHT FINISH		☐ PARAGLIDER	☐ HARNESS
SLOPE GRADIENT	↑ ↓	☐ GOGGLES	☐ HELMET
		☐ RESERVE	☐ GLOVES

LAUNCH LOCATION	LANDING LOCATION

NOTES & OBSERVATIONS

_____

_____

_____

AIRTIME DURATION		FLIGHT CENTER STAMP	
TODAY			☐ INSTRUCTOR
TO DATE			☐ FLIGHT TUTOR
ALL TIME			☐ FLIGHT BUDDY

SIGNATURE _____

LOCATION		DATE
PARAGLIDER		
PARAMOTOR		/ /

LAUNCH TYPE		AIRTIME	
		AIR DISTANCE	

WEATHER CONDITION	☀ ☁ ❄ ⛈ 🌬	TIME OF YEAR	🌷 ☀ 🍃 ❄

FLIGHT START	🕐	GEAR CHECKLIST	
FLIGHT FINISH		☐ PARAGLIDER	☐ HARNESS
SLOPE GRADIENT	↑↓	☐ GOGGLES	☐ HELMET
		☐ RESERVE	☐ GLOVES

LAUNCH LOCATION	LANDING LOCATION

NOTES & OBSERVATIONS

_____

_____

_____

AIRTIME DURATION		FLIGHT CENTER STAMP	
TODAY			☐ INSTRUCTOR
TO DATE			☐ FLIGHT TUTOR
ALL TIME			☐ FLIGHT BUDDY

SIGNATURE _____

LOCATION		DATE	
PARAGLIDER			
PARAMOTOR		/ /	

LAUNCH TYPE		AIRTIME	
		AIR DISTANCE	

WEATHER CONDITION	☀ ☂ ❄ ⚡ ≈	TIME OF YEAR	❀ ☀ 🍂 ❄

FLIGHT START	🕐		GEAR CHECKLIST	
FLIGHT FINISH		☐ PARAGLIDER	☐ HARNESS
SLOPE GRADIENT	↕	☐ GOGGLES	☐ HELMET
		☐ RESERVE	☐ GLOVES

LAUNCH LOCATION	LANDING LOCATION

NOTES & OBSERVATIONS

_____

_____

_____

AIRTIME DURATION		FLIGHT CENTER STAMP	
TODAY			☐ INSTRUCTOR
TO DATE			☐ FLIGHT TUTOR
ALL TIME			☐ FLIGHT BUDDY

SIGNATURE

_____

LOCATION		DATE
PARAGLIDER		
PARAMOTOR		/ /

LAUNCH TYPE		AIRTIME	
		AIR DISTANCE	

WEATHER CONDITION	☀ ☁ ❄ ⛈ 🌬	TIME OF YEAR	🌷 ☀ 🍃 ❄

FLIGHT START	🕐	GEAR CHECKLIST	
FLIGHT FINISH		☐ PARAGLIDER	☐ HARNESS
SLOPE GRADIENT	⬆⬇	☐ GOGGLES	☐ HELMET
		☐ RESERVE	☐ GLOVES

LAUNCH LOCATION	LANDING LOCATION

NOTES & OBSERVATIONS

_____

_____

_____

AIRTIME DURATION		FLIGHT CENTER STAMP	
TODAY			☐ INSTRUCTOR
TO DATE			☐ FLIGHT TUTOR
ALL TIME			☐ FLIGHT BUDDY

SIGNATURE

_____

LOCATION		DATE	
PARAGLIDER			
PARAMOTOR		/ /	

LAUNCH TYPE		AIRTIME	
		AIR DISTANCE	

WEATHER CONDITION	☀ ☁ ❄ ⛈ 🌬	TIME OF YEAR	🌷 ☀ 🍂 ❄

FLIGHT START	🕐	GEAR CHECKLIST	
FLIGHT FINISH		☐ PARAGLIDER ☐ HARNESS	
SLOPE GRADIENT	↕	☐ GOGGLES ☐ HELMET	
		☐ RESERVE ☐ GLOVES	

LAUNCH LOCATION	LANDING LOCATION

NOTES & OBSERVATIONS

AIRTIME DURATION		FLIGHT CENTER STAMP	
TODAY			☐ INSTRUCTOR
TO DATE			☐ FLIGHT TUTOR
ALL TIME			☐ FLIGHT BUDDY

SIGNATURE

LOCATION		DATE
PARAGLIDER		
PARAMOTOR		/ /

LAUNCH TYPE		AIRTIME	
		AIR DISTANCE	

WEATHER CONDITION	☀ ☁ ❄ ⛈ 🌬	TIME OF YEAR	🌷 ☀ 🍃 ❄

FLIGHT START	🕐	GEAR CHECKLIST	
FLIGHT FINISH		☐ PARAGLIDER	☐ HARNESS
SLOPE GRADIENT	↕	☐ GOGGLES	☐ HELMET
		☐ RESERVE	☐ GLOVES

LAUNCH LOCATION	LANDING LOCATION

NOTES & OBSERVATIONS

_____

_____

_____

AIRTIME DURATION		FLIGHT CENTER STAMP	
TODAY			☐ INSTRUCTOR
TO DATE			☐ FLIGHT TUTOR
ALL TIME			☐ FLIGHT BUDDY

SIGNATURE

_____

LOCATION		DATE
PARAGLIDER		
PARAMOTOR		/ /

LAUNCH TYPE		AIRTIME	
		AIR DISTANCE	

WEATHER CONDITION	☀ ☁ ❄ ⛈ 💨	TIME OF YEAR	🌷 ☀ 🍃 ❄

FLIGHT START	🕐	GEAR CHECKLIST	
FLIGHT FINISH		☐ PARAGLIDER	☐ HARNESS
SLOPE GRADIENT	↑ ↓	☐ GOGGLES	☐ HELMET
		☐ RESERVE	☐ GLOVES

LAUNCH LOCATION	LANDING LOCATION

NOTES & OBSERVATIONS

_____

_____

_____

AIRTIME DURATION		FLIGHT CENTER STAMP	
TODAY			☐ INSTRUCTOR
TO DATE			☐ FLIGHT TUTOR
ALL TIME			☐ FLIGHT BUDDY

SIGNATURE

_____

LOCATION		DATE
PARAGLIDER		
PARAMOTOR		/ /

LAUNCH TYPE		AIRTIME	
		AIR DISTANCE	

WEATHER CONDITION	☀ ☁ ❄ ⛈ 🌬	TIME OF YEAR	🌷 ☀ 🍃 ❄

FLIGHT START	🕐	GEAR CHECKLIST	
FLIGHT FINISH		☐ PARAGLIDER	☐ HARNESS
SLOPE GRADIENT	↑ ↓	☐ GOGGLES	☐ HELMET
		☐ RESERVE	☐ GLOVES

LAUNCH LOCATION	LANDING LOCATION

NOTES & OBSERVATIONS

_____

_____

_____

AIRTIME DURATION		FLIGHT CENTER STAMP	
TODAY			☐ INSTRUCTOR
TO DATE			☐ FLIGHT TUTOR
ALL TIME			☐ FLIGHT BUDDY

SIGNATURE

_____

LOCATION		DATE	
PARAGLIDER			
PARAMOTOR		/ /	

LAUNCH TYPE		AIRTIME	
		AIR DISTANCE	

WEATHER CONDITION	☀ ☁ ❄ ⛈ 🌬	TIME OF YEAR	🌷 ☀ 🍁 ❄

FLIGHT START	🕐	GEAR CHECKLIST	
FLIGHT FINISH		☐ PARAGLIDER	☐ HARNESS
SLOPE GRADIENT	↑ ↓	☐ GOGGLES	☐ HELMET
		☐ RESERVE	☐ GLOVES

LAUNCH LOCATION	LANDING LOCATION

NOTES & OBSERVATIONS

_____

_____

_____

AIRTIME DURATION		FLIGHT CENTER STAMP	
TODAY			☐ INSTRUCTOR
TO DATE			☐ FLIGHT TUTOR
ALL TIME			☐ FLIGHT BUDDY

SIGNATURE

_____

LOCATION		DATE
PARAGLIDER		
PARAMOTOR		/ /

LAUNCH TYPE		AIRTIME	
		AIR DISTANCE	

WEATHER CONDITION	☀ ☁ ❄ ⛈ 🌬	TIME OF YEAR	🌷 ☀ 🍃 ❄

FLIGHT START	🕐	GEAR CHECKLIST	
FLIGHT FINISH		☐ PARAGLIDER	☐ HARNESS
SLOPE GRADIENT	↑↓	☐ GOGGLES	☐ HELMET
		☐ RESERVE	☐ GLOVES

LAUNCH LOCATION	LANDING LOCATION

NOTES & OBSERVATIONS

_____

_____

_____

AIRTIME DURATION		FLIGHT CENTER STAMP	
TODAY			☐ INSTRUCTOR
TO DATE			☐ FLIGHT TUTOR
ALL TIME			☐ FLIGHT BUDDY

SIGNATURE
_____

LOCATION		DATE
PARAGLIDER		
PARAMOTOR		/ /

LAUNCH TYPE		AIRTIME	
		AIR DISTANCE	

WEATHER CONDITION	☀ ☁ ❄ ⛈ 🌬	TIME OF YEAR	🌷 ☀ 🍁 ❄

FLIGHT START	🕐		GEAR CHECKLIST	
FLIGHT FINISH			☐ PARAGLIDER	☐ HARNESS
SLOPE GRADIENT	↑ ↓		☐ GOGGLES	☐ HELMET
			☐ RESERVE	☐ GLOVES

LAUNCH LOCATION

LANDING LOCATION

NOTES & OBSERVATIONS

_____

_____

_____

AIRTIME DURATION		FLIGHT CENTER STAMP	
TODAY			☐ INSTRUCTOR
TO DATE			☐ FLIGHT TUTOR
ALL TIME			☐ FLIGHT BUDDY

SIGNATURE

_____

LOCATION		DATE
PARAGLIDER		
PARAMOTOR		/ /

LAUNCH TYPE		AIRTIME	
		AIR DISTANCE	

WEATHER CONDITION	☀ ☁ ❄ ⛈ 🌬	TIME OF YEAR	🌷 ☀ 🍃 ❄

FLIGHT START	🕐	GEAR CHECKLIST	
FLIGHT FINISH		☐ PARAGLIDER	☐ HARNESS
SLOPE GRADIENT	↑↓	☐ GOGGLES	☐ HELMET
		☐ RESERVE	☐ GLOVES

LAUNCH LOCATION	LANDING LOCATION

NOTES & OBSERVATIONS

_____

_____

_____

AIRTIME DURATION		FLIGHT CENTER STAMP
TODAY		☐ INSTRUCTOR
TO DATE		☐ FLIGHT TUTOR
ALL TIME		☐ FLIGHT BUDDY

SIGNATURE

_____

LOCATION		DATE
PARAGLIDER		
PARAMOTOR		/ /

LAUNCH TYPE		AIRTIME	
		AIR DISTANCE	

WEATHER CONDITION	☀ ☁ ❄ ⛈ 💨	TIME OF YEAR	🌷 ☀ 🍁 ❄

FLIGHT START	🕐	GEAR CHECKLIST	
FLIGHT FINISH		☐ PARAGLIDER	☐ HARNESS
SLOPE GRADIENT	↑ ↓	☐ GOGGLES	☐ HELMET
		☐ RESERVE	☐ GLOVES

LAUNCH LOCATION	LANDING LOCATION

NOTES & OBSERVATIONS

_____

_____

_____

AIRTIME DURATION		FLIGHT CENTER STAMP	
TODAY			☐ INSTRUCTOR
TO DATE			☐ FLIGHT TUTOR
ALL TIME			☐ FLIGHT BUDDY

SIGNATURE _____

LOCATION		DATE
PARAGLIDER		
PARAMOTOR		/ /

LAUNCH TYPE		AIRTIME	
		AIR DISTANCE	

WEATHER CONDITION	☀ ☁ ❄ ⛈ 🌬	TIME OF YEAR	🌷 ☀ 🍃 ❄

FLIGHT START	🕐	GEAR CHECKLIST	
FLIGHT FINISH		☐ PARAGLIDER	☐ HARNESS
SLOPE GRADIENT	↑ ↓	☐ GOGGLES	☐ HELMET
		☐ RESERVE	☐ GLOVES

LAUNCH LOCATION	LANDING LOCATION

NOTES & OBSERVATIONS

_____

_____

_____

AIRTIME DURATION		FLIGHT CENTER STAMP	
TODAY			☐ INSTRUCTOR
TO DATE			☐ FLIGHT TUTOR
ALL TIME			☐ FLIGHT BUDDY

SIGNATURE _____

LOCATION		DATE
PARAGLIDER		
PARAMOTOR		/ /

LAUNCH TYPE		AIRTIME	
		AIR DISTANCE	

WEATHER CONDITION	☀ ☁ ❄ ⛈ 💨	TIME OF YEAR	🌷 ☀ 🍂 ❄

FLIGHT START	🕐	GEAR CHECKLIST	
FLIGHT FINISH		☐ PARAGLIDER	☐ HARNESS
SLOPE GRADIENT	↑ ↓	☐ GOGGLES	☐ HELMET
		☐ RESERVE	☐ GLOVES

LAUNCH LOCATION	LANDING LOCATION

NOTES & OBSERVATIONS

_____

_____

_____

AIRTIME DURATION		FLIGHT CENTER STAMP	
TODAY			☐ INSTRUCTOR
TO DATE			☐ FLIGHT TUTOR
ALL TIME			☐ FLIGHT BUDDY

SIGNATURE _____

LOCATION		DATE
PARAGLIDER		
PARAMOTOR		/ /

LAUNCH TYPE		AIRTIME	
		AIR DISTANCE	

WEATHER CONDITION	☀ ☁ ❄ ⛈ 🌬	TIME OF YEAR	🌷 ☀ 🍃 ❄

FLIGHT START	🕐	GEAR CHECKLIST	
FLIGHT FINISH		☐ PARAGLIDER ☐ HARNESS	
SLOPE GRADIENT	↑↓	☐ GOGGLES ☐ HELMET	
		☐ RESERVE ☐ GLOVES	

LAUNCH LOCATION	LANDING LOCATION

NOTES & OBSERVATIONS

_____

_____

_____

AIRTIME DURATION		FLIGHT CENTER STAMP	
TODAY			☐ INSTRUCTOR
TO DATE			☐ FLIGHT TUTOR
ALL TIME			☐ FLIGHT BUDDY

SIGNATURE _____

LOCATION		DATE
PARAGLIDER		
PARAMOTOR		/ /

LAUNCH TYPE		AIRTIME	
		AIR DISTANCE	

WEATHER CONDITION	☀ ☁ ❄ ⛈ 🌬	TIME OF YEAR	🌷 ☀ 🍁 ❄

FLIGHT START	🕐	GEAR CHECKLIST	
FLIGHT FINISH		☐ PARAGLIDER	☐ HARNESS
SLOPE GRADIENT	↑ ↓	☐ GOGGLES	☐ HELMET
		☐ RESERVE	☐ GLOVES

LAUNCH LOCATION	LANDING LOCATION

NOTES & OBSERVATIONS

_____

_____

_____

AIRTIME DURATION		FLIGHT CENTER STAMP	
TODAY			☐ INSTRUCTOR
TO DATE			☐ FLIGHT TUTOR
ALL TIME			☐ FLIGHT BUDDY

SIGNATURE

_____

LOCATION		DATE
PARAGLIDER		
PARAMOTOR		/ /

LAUNCH TYPE		AIRTIME	
		AIR DISTANCE	

WEATHER CONDITION	☀ ☁ ❄ ⛈ 🌬	TIME OF YEAR	🌷 ☀ 🍃 ❄

FLIGHT START	🕐	GEAR CHECKLIST	
FLIGHT FINISH		☐ PARAGLIDER	☐ HARNESS
SLOPE GRADIENT	↑↓	☐ GOGGLES	☐ HELMET
		☐ RESERVE	☐ GLOVES

LAUNCH LOCATION	LANDING LOCATION

NOTES & OBSERVATIONS

_____

_____

_____

AIRTIME DURATION		FLIGHT CENTER STAMP	
TODAY			☐ INSTRUCTOR
TO DATE			☐ FLIGHT TUTOR
ALL TIME			☐ FLIGHT BUDDY

SIGNATURE _____

LOCATION		DATE
PARAGLIDER		
PARAMOTOR		/ /

LAUNCH TYPE		AIRTIME	
		AIR DISTANCE	

WEATHER CONDITION	☀ ☁ ❄ ⛈ 🌬	TIME OF YEAR	🌷 ☀ 🍃 ❄

FLIGHT START	🕐	GEAR CHECKLIST	
FLIGHT FINISH		☐ PARAGLIDER	☐ HARNESS
SLOPE GRADIENT	↑ ↓	☐ GOGGLES	☐ HELMET
		☐ RESERVE	☐ GLOVES

LAUNCH LOCATION	LANDING LOCATION

NOTES & OBSERVATIONS

_____

_____

_____

AIRTIME DURATION		FLIGHT CENTER STAMP	
TODAY			☐ INSTRUCTOR
TO DATE			☐ FLIGHT TUTOR
ALL TIME			☐ FLIGHT BUDDY

SIGNATURE

_____

LOCATION		DATE
PARAGLIDER		
PARAMOTOR		/ /

LAUNCH TYPE		AIRTIME	
		AIR DISTANCE	

WEATHER CONDITION	☀ ☁ ❄ 🌧 ≈	TIME OF YEAR	🌷 ☀ 🍃 ❄

FLIGHT START	🕐	GEAR CHECKLIST	
FLIGHT FINISH		☐ PARAGLIDER	☐ HARNESS
SLOPE GRADIENT	↑ ↓	☐ GOGGLES	☐ HELMET
		☐ RESERVE	☐ GLOVES

LAUNCH LOCATION	LANDING LOCATION

NOTES & OBSERVATIONS

_____

_____

_____

AIRTIME DURATION		FLIGHT CENTER STAMP	
TODAY			☐ INSTRUCTOR
TO DATE			☐ FLIGHT TUTOR
ALL TIME			☐ FLIGHT BUDDY

SIGNATURE

_____

LOCATION		DATE	
PARAGLIDER			
PARAMOTOR		/ /	

LAUNCH TYPE		AIRTIME	
		AIR DISTANCE	

WEATHER CONDITION	☀ ☁ ❄ ⛈ 🌬	TIME OF YEAR	🌷 ☀ 🍃 ❄

FLIGHT START	🕐	GEAR CHECKLIST	
FLIGHT FINISH		☐ PARAGLIDER	☐ HARNESS
SLOPE GRADIENT	↑ ↓	☐ GOGGLES	☐ HELMET
		☐ RESERVE	☐ GLOVES

LAUNCH LOCATION	LANDING LOCATION

NOTES & OBSERVATIONS

_____

_____

_____

AIRTIME DURATION		FLIGHT CENTER STAMP	
TODAY			☐ INSTRUCTOR
TO DATE			☐ FLIGHT TUTOR
ALL TIME			☐ FLIGHT BUDDY

SIGNATURE

_____

LOCATION		DATE
PARAGLIDER		
PARAMOTOR		/ /

LAUNCH TYPE		AIRTIME	
		AIR DISTANCE	

WEATHER CONDITION	☀ ☁ ❄ ⛈ 🌬	TIME OF YEAR	🌷 ☀ 🍃 ❄

FLIGHT START	🕐	GEAR CHECKLIST	
FLIGHT FINISH		☐ PARAGLIDER	☐ HARNESS
SLOPE GRADIENT	⬆⬇	☐ GOGGLES	☐ HELMET
		☐ RESERVE	☐ GLOVES

LAUNCH LOCATION	LANDING LOCATION

NOTES & OBSERVATIONS

_____

_____

_____

AIRTIME DURATION		FLIGHT CENTER STAMP	
TODAY			☐ INSTRUCTOR
TO DATE			☐ FLIGHT TUTOR
ALL TIME			☐ FLIGHT BUDDY

SIGNATURE

_____

LOCATION		DATE
PARAGLIDER		
PARAMOTOR		/ /

LAUNCH TYPE		AIRTIME	
		AIR DISTANCE	

WEATHER CONDITION	☀ ☁ ❄ ⛈ 🌬	TIME OF YEAR	🌷 ☀ 🍃 ❄

FLIGHT START	🕐	GEAR CHECKLIST	
FLIGHT FINISH		☐ PARAGLIDER	☐ HARNESS
SLOPE GRADIENT	↕	☐ GOGGLES	☐ HELMET
		☐ RESERVE	☐ GLOVES

LAUNCH LOCATION	LANDING LOCATION

NOTES & OBSERVATIONS

_____

_____

_____

AIRTIME DURATION		FLIGHT CENTER STAMP	
TODAY			☐ INSTRUCTOR
TO DATE			☐ FLIGHT TUTOR
ALL TIME			☐ FLIGHT BUDDY

SIGNATURE _____

LOCATION		DATE
PARAGLIDER		
PARAMOTOR		/ /

LAUNCH TYPE		AIRTIME	
		AIR DISTANCE	

WEATHER CONDITION	☀ ☁ ❄ ⛈ 🌬	TIME OF YEAR	🌷 ☀ 🍃 ❄

FLIGHT START	🕐	GEAR CHECKLIST	
FLIGHT FINISH		☐ PARAGLIDER	☐ HARNESS
SLOPE GRADIENT	↑ ↓	☐ GOGGLES	☐ HELMET
		☐ RESERVE	☐ GLOVES

LAUNCH LOCATION	LANDING LOCATION

NOTES & OBSERVATIONS

_____

_____

_____

AIRTIME DURATION		FLIGHT CENTER STAMP	
TODAY			☐ INSTRUCTOR
TO DATE			☐ FLIGHT TUTOR
ALL TIME			☐ FLIGHT BUDDY

SIGNATURE _____

LOCATION		DATE
PARAGLIDER		
PARAMOTOR		/ /

LAUNCH TYPE		AIRTIME	
		AIR DISTANCE	

WEATHER CONDITION	☀ ☁ ❄ ⛈ 🌬	TIME OF YEAR	🌷 ☀ 🍂 ❄

FLIGHT START	🕐	GEAR CHECKLIST	
FLIGHT FINISH		☐ PARAGLIDER	☐ HARNESS
SLOPE GRADIENT	↑ ↓	☐ GOGGLES	☐ HELMET
		☐ RESERVE	☐ GLOVES

LAUNCH LOCATION	LANDING LOCATION

NOTES & OBSERVATIONS

_____

_____

_____

AIRTIME DURATION		FLIGHT CENTER STAMP	
TODAY			☐ INSTRUCTOR
TO DATE			☐ FLIGHT TUTOR
ALL TIME			☐ FLIGHT BUDDY

SIGNATURE _____

LOCATION		DATE
PARAGLIDER		
PARAMOTOR		/ /

LAUNCH TYPE		AIRTIME	
		AIR DISTANCE	

WEATHER CONDITION	☀ ☁ ❄ ⛈ 🌬	TIME OF YEAR	🌷 ☀ 🍃 ❄

FLIGHT START	🕐	GEAR CHECKLIST	
FLIGHT FINISH		☐ PARAGLIDER	☐ HARNESS
SLOPE GRADIENT	↑ ↓	☐ GOGGLES	☐ HELMET
		☐ RESERVE	☐ GLOVES

LAUNCH LOCATION	LANDING LOCATION

NOTES & OBSERVATIONS

AIRTIME DURATION

TODAY	
TO DATE	
ALL TIME	

FLIGHT CENTER STAMP

☐ INSTRUCTOR

☐ FLIGHT TUTOR

☐ FLIGHT BUDDY

SIGNATURE

LOCATION		DATE
PARAGLIDER		
PARAMOTOR		/ /

LAUNCH TYPE		AIRTIME	
		AIR DISTANCE	

WEATHER CONDITION	☀ ☂ ❄ ⛈ 🌬	TIME OF YEAR	🌷 ☀ 🍂 ❄

FLIGHT START	🕐	GEAR CHECKLIST	
FLIGHT FINISH		☐ PARAGLIDER	☐ HARNESS
SLOPE GRADIENT	↑ ↓	☐ GOGGLES	☐ HELMET
		☐ RESERVE	☐ GLOVES

LAUNCH LOCATION	LANDING LOCATION

NOTES & OBSERVATIONS

_____

_____

_____

AIRTIME DURATION		FLIGHT CENTER STAMP	
TODAY			☐ INSTRUCTOR
TO DATE			☐ FLIGHT TUTOR
ALL TIME			☐ FLIGHT BUDDY

SIGNATURE

_____

LOCATION		DATE
PARAGLIDER		
PARAMOTOR		/ /

LAUNCH TYPE		AIRTIME	
		AIR DISTANCE	

WEATHER CONDITION	☀ ☁ ❄ ⛈ 🌬	TIME OF YEAR	🌷 ☀ 🍁 ❄

FLIGHT START	🕐	GEAR CHECKLIST	
FLIGHT FINISH		☐ PARAGLIDER	☐ HARNESS
SLOPE GRADIENT	⬆ ⬇	☐ GOGGLES	☐ HELMET
		☐ RESERVE	☐ GLOVES

LAUNCH LOCATION	LANDING LOCATION

NOTES & OBSERVATIONS

_____

_____

_____

AIRTIME DURATION		FLIGHT CENTER STAMP
TODAY		
TO DATE		☐ INSTRUCTOR
ALL TIME		☐ FLIGHT TUTOR
		☐ FLIGHT BUDDY

SIGNATURE

_____

LOCATION		DATE
PARAGLIDER		
PARAMOTOR		/ /

LAUNCH TYPE		AIRTIME	
		AIR DISTANCE	

WEATHER CONDITION	☀ 🌧 ❄ ⛈ 💨	TIME OF YEAR	🌷 ☀ 🍁 ❄

FLIGHT START	🕐	GEAR CHECKLIST	
FLIGHT FINISH		☐ PARAGLIDER	☐ HARNESS
SLOPE GRADIENT	↕	☐ GOGGLES	☐ HELMET
		☐ RESERVE	☐ GLOVES

LAUNCH LOCATION	LANDING LOCATION

NOTES & OBSERVATIONS

_____

_____

_____

AIRTIME DURATION		FLIGHT CENTER STAMP	
TODAY			☐ INSTRUCTOR
TO DATE			☐ FLIGHT TUTOR
ALL TIME			☐ FLIGHT BUDDY

SIGNATURE

_____

LOCATION		DATE
PARAGLIDER		
PARAMOTOR		/ /

LAUNCH TYPE		AIRTIME	
		AIR DISTANCE	

WEATHER CONDITION	☀ ☁ ❄ ⛈ 🌬	TIME OF YEAR	🌷 ☀ 🍁 ❄

FLIGHT START	🕐	GEAR CHECKLIST	
FLIGHT FINISH		☐ PARAGLIDER	☐ HARNESS
SLOPE GRADIENT	↑↓	☐ GOGGLES	☐ HELMET
		☐ RESERVE	☐ GLOVES

LAUNCH LOCATION	LANDING LOCATION

NOTES & OBSERVATIONS

_____

_____

_____

AIRTIME DURATION		FLIGHT CENTER STAMP	
TODAY			☐ INSTRUCTOR
TO DATE			☐ FLIGHT TUTOR
ALL TIME			☐ FLIGHT BUDDY

SIGNATURE _____

LOCATION		DATE
PARAGLIDER		
PARAMOTOR		/ /

LAUNCH TYPE		AIRTIME	
		AIR DISTANCE	

WEATHER CONDITION	☀ ☁ ❄ ⛈ 🌬	TIME OF YEAR	🌷 ☀ 🍂 ❄

FLIGHT START	🕐	GEAR CHECKLIST	
FLIGHT FINISH		☐ PARAGLIDER	☐ HARNESS
SLOPE GRADIENT	↑ ↓	☐ GOGGLES	☐ HELMET
		☐ RESERVE	☐ GLOVES

LAUNCH LOCATION	LANDING LOCATION

NOTES & OBSERVATIONS

_____

_____

_____

AIRTIME DURATION		FLIGHT CENTER STAMP	
TODAY			☐ INSTRUCTOR
TO DATE			☐ FLIGHT TUTOR
ALL TIME			☐ FLIGHT BUDDY

SIGNATURE

_____

LOCATION		DATE
PARAGLIDER		
PARAMOTOR		/ /

LAUNCH TYPE		AIRTIME	
		AIR DISTANCE	

WEATHER CONDITION	☀ ☁ ❄ ⛈ 🌬	TIME OF YEAR	🌷 ☀ 🍃 ❄

FLIGHT START	🕐	GEAR CHECKLIST	
FLIGHT FINISH		☐ PARAGLIDER	☐ HARNESS
SLOPE GRADIENT	↑↓	☐ GOGGLES	☐ HELMET
		☐ RESERVE	☐ GLOVES

LAUNCH LOCATION	LANDING LOCATION

NOTES & OBSERVATIONS

AIRTIME DURATION		FLIGHT CENTER STAMP	
TODAY			☐ INSTRUCTOR
TO DATE			☐ FLIGHT TUTOR
ALL TIME			☐ FLIGHT BUDDY

SIGNATURE

LOCATION		DATE
PARAGLIDER		
PARAMOTOR		/ /

LAUNCH TYPE		AIRTIME	
		AIR DISTANCE	

WEATHER CONDITION	☀ ☁ ❄ ⛈ 🌬	TIME OF YEAR	🌷 ☀ 🍁 ❄

FLIGHT START	🕐	GEAR CHECKLIST	
FLIGHT FINISH		☐ PARAGLIDER	☐ HARNESS
SLOPE GRADIENT	↑ ↓	☐ GOGGLES	☐ HELMET
		☐ RESERVE	☐ GLOVES

LAUNCH LOCATION	LANDING LOCATION

NOTES & OBSERVATIONS

_____

_____

_____

AIRTIME DURATION		FLIGHT CENTER STAMP	
TODAY			☐ INSTRUCTOR
TO DATE			☐ FLIGHT TUTOR
ALL TIME			☐ FLIGHT BUDDY

SIGNATURE

_____

LOCATION		DATE
PARAGLIDER		
PARAMOTOR		/ /

LAUNCH TYPE		AIRTIME	
		AIR DISTANCE	

WEATHER CONDITION	☀ ☁ ❄ ⚡ 🌬	TIME OF YEAR	🌷 ☀ 🍃 ❄

FLIGHT START	🕐	GEAR CHECKLIST	
FLIGHT FINISH		☐ PARAGLIDER	☐ HARNESS
SLOPE GRADIENT	⬆⬇	☐ GOGGLES	☐ HELMET
		☐ RESERVE	☐ GLOVES

LAUNCH LOCATION	LANDING LOCATION

NOTES & OBSERVATIONS

_____

_____

_____

AIRTIME DURATION		FLIGHT CENTER STAMP	
TODAY			☐ INSTRUCTOR
TO DATE			☐ FLIGHT TUTOR
ALL TIME			☐ FLIGHT BUDDY

SIGNATURE

_____

LOCATION		DATE
PARAGLIDER		
PARAMOTOR		/ /

LAUNCH TYPE		AIRTIME	
		AIR DISTANCE	

WEATHER CONDITION	☀ ☔ ❄ ⛈ 🌬	TIME OF YEAR	🌷 ☀ 🍁 ❄

FLIGHT START	🕐	GEAR CHECKLIST	
FLIGHT FINISH		☐ PARAGLIDER	☐ HARNESS
SLOPE GRADIENT	↑ ↓	☐ GOGGLES	☐ HELMET
		☐ RESERVE	☐ GLOVES

LAUNCH LOCATION	LANDING LOCATION

NOTES & OBSERVATIONS

_____

_____

_____

AIRTIME DURATION		FLIGHT CENTER STAMP	
TODAY			☐ INSTRUCTOR
TO DATE			☐ FLIGHT TUTOR
ALL TIME			☐ FLIGHT BUDDY

SIGNATURE _____

LOCATION		DATE
PARAGLIDER		
PARAMOTOR		/ /

LAUNCH TYPE		AIRTIME	
		AIR DISTANCE	

WEATHER CONDITION	☀ ☁ ❄ ⛈ 🌬	TIME OF YEAR	🌷 ☀ 🍃 ❄

FLIGHT START	🕐	GEAR CHECKLIST	
FLIGHT FINISH		☐ PARAGLIDER	☐ HARNESS
SLOPE GRADIENT	↑ ↓	☐ GOGGLES	☐ HELMET
		☐ RESERVE	☐ GLOVES

LAUNCH LOCATION	LANDING LOCATION

NOTES & OBSERVATIONS

_____

_____

_____

AIRTIME DURATION		FLIGHT CENTER STAMP	
TODAY			☐ INSTRUCTOR
TO DATE			☐ FLIGHT TUTOR
ALL TIME			☐ FLIGHT BUDDY

SIGNATURE

_____

LOCATION		DATE
PARAGLIDER		
PARAMOTOR		/ /

LAUNCH TYPE		AIRTIME	
		AIR DISTANCE	

WEATHER CONDITION	☀ ☁ ❄ ⛈ 🌬	TIME OF YEAR	🌷 ☀ 🍃 ❄

FLIGHT START	🕐	GEAR CHECKLIST	
FLIGHT FINISH		☐ PARAGLIDER	☐ HARNESS
SLOPE GRADIENT	↑ ↓	☐ GOGGLES	☐ HELMET
		☐ RESERVE	☐ GLOVES

LAUNCH LOCATION	LANDING LOCATION

NOTES & OBSERVATIONS

_____

_____

_____

AIRTIME DURATION		FLIGHT CENTER STAMP	
TODAY			☐ INSTRUCTOR
TO DATE			☐ FLIGHT TUTOR
ALL TIME			☐ FLIGHT BUDDY

SIGNATURE _____

LOCATION		DATE
PARAGLIDER		
PARAMOTOR		/ /

LAUNCH TYPE		AIRTIME	
		AIR DISTANCE	

WEATHER CONDITION	☀ ☁ ❄ ⛈ 💨	TIME OF YEAR	🌷 ☀ 🍃 ❄

FLIGHT START	🕐	GEAR CHECKLIST	
FLIGHT FINISH		☐ PARAGLIDER ☐ HARNESS	
SLOPE GRADIENT	↑↓	☐ GOGGLES ☐ HELMET	
		☐ RESERVE ☐ GLOVES	

LAUNCH LOCATION	LANDING LOCATION

NOTES & OBSERVATIONS

AIRTIME DURATION		FLIGHT CENTER STAMP	
TODAY			☐ INSTRUCTOR
TO DATE			☐ FLIGHT TUTOR
ALL TIME			☐ FLIGHT BUDDY

SIGNATURE

LOCATION		DATE
PARAGLIDER		
PARAMOTOR		/ /

LAUNCH TYPE		AIRTIME	
		AIR DISTANCE	

WEATHER CONDITION	☀ ☁ ❄ ⛈ 💨	TIME OF YEAR	🌷 ☀ 🍁 ❄

FLIGHT START	🕐	GEAR CHECKLIST	
FLIGHT FINISH		☐ PARAGLIDER	☐ HARNESS
SLOPE GRADIENT	↑ ↓	☐ GOGGLES	☐ HELMET
		☐ RESERVE	☐ GLOVES

LAUNCH LOCATION	LANDING LOCATION

NOTES & OBSERVATIONS

_____

_____

_____

AIRTIME DURATION		FLIGHT CENTER STAMP	
TODAY			☐ INSTRUCTOR
TO DATE			☐ FLIGHT TUTOR
ALL TIME			☐ FLIGHT BUDDY

SIGNATURE _____

LOCATION		DATE
PARAGLIDER		
PARAMOTOR		/ /

LAUNCH TYPE		AIRTIME	
		AIR DISTANCE	

WEATHER CONDITION	☀ ☁ ❄ ⛈ 🌬	TIME OF YEAR	🌷 ☀ 🍂 ❄

FLIGHT START	🕐	GEAR CHECKLIST	
FLIGHT FINISH		☐ PARAGLIDER	☐ HARNESS
SLOPE GRADIENT	↑↓	☐ GOGGLES	☐ HELMET
		☐ RESERVE	☐ GLOVES

LAUNCH LOCATION	LANDING LOCATION

NOTES & OBSERVATIONS

_____

_____

_____

AIRTIME DURATION		FLIGHT CENTER STAMP
TODAY		☐ INSTRUCTOR
TO DATE		☐ FLIGHT TUTOR
ALL TIME		☐ FLIGHT BUDDY

SIGNATURE

_____

LOCATION		DATE
PARAGLIDER		
PARAMOTOR		/ /

LAUNCH TYPE		AIRTIME	
		AIR DISTANCE	

WEATHER CONDITION	☀ ☁ ❄ ⛈ 🌬	TIME OF YEAR	🌷 ☀ 🍁 ❄

FLIGHT START	🕐	GEAR CHECKLIST	
FLIGHT FINISH		☐ PARAGLIDER	☐ HARNESS
SLOPE GRADIENT	↑ ↓	☐ GOGGLES	☐ HELMET
		☐ RESERVE	☐ GLOVES

LAUNCH LOCATION	LANDING LOCATION

NOTES & OBSERVATIONS

_____

_____

_____

AIRTIME DURATION		FLIGHT CENTER STAMP	
TODAY			☐ INSTRUCTOR
TO DATE			☐ FLIGHT TUTOR
ALL TIME			☐ FLIGHT BUDDY

SIGNATURE

_____

LOCATION		DATE
PARAGLIDER		
PARAMOTOR		/ /

LAUNCH TYPE		AIRTIME	
		AIR DISTANCE	

WEATHER CONDITION	☀ ☁ ❄ ⛈ 💨	TIME OF YEAR	🌷 ☀ 🍁 ❄

FLIGHT START	🕐	GEAR CHECKLIST	
FLIGHT FINISH		☐ PARAGLIDER	☐ HARNESS
SLOPE GRADIENT	↑↓	☐ GOGGLES	☐ HELMET
		☐ RESERVE	☐ GLOVES

LAUNCH LOCATION	LANDING LOCATION

NOTES & OBSERVATIONS

_____

_____

_____

AIRTIME DURATION		FLIGHT CENTER STAMP	
TODAY			☐ INSTRUCTOR
TO DATE			☐ FLIGHT TUTOR
ALL TIME			☐ FLIGHT BUDDY

SIGNATURE _____

LOCATION		DATE
PARAGLIDER		
PARAMOTOR		/ /

LAUNCH TYPE		AIRTIME	
		AIR DISTANCE	

WEATHER CONDITION	☀ ☁ ❄ ⛈ 🌬	TIME OF YEAR	🌷 ☀ 🍂 ❄

FLIGHT START	🕐	GEAR CHECKLIST	
FLIGHT FINISH		☐ PARAGLIDER	☐ HARNESS
SLOPE GRADIENT	↑ ↓	☐ GOGGLES	☐ HELMET
		☐ RESERVE	☐ GLOVES

LAUNCH LOCATION	LANDING LOCATION

NOTES & OBSERVATIONS

_____

_____

_____

AIRTIME DURATION		FLIGHT CENTER STAMP	
TODAY			☐ INSTRUCTOR
TO DATE			☐ FLIGHT TUTOR
ALL TIME			☐ FLIGHT BUDDY

SIGNATURE _____

LOCATION		DATE
PARAGLIDER		
PARAMOTOR		/ /

LAUNCH TYPE		AIRTIME	
		AIR DISTANCE	

WEATHER CONDITION	☀ ☁ ❄ ⛈ 💨	TIME OF YEAR	🌷 ☀ 🍃 ❄

FLIGHT START	🕐	GEAR CHECKLIST	
FLIGHT FINISH		☐ PARAGLIDER	☐ HARNESS
SLOPE GRADIENT	↑ ↓	☐ GOGGLES	☐ HELMET
		☐ RESERVE	☐ GLOVES

LAUNCH LOCATION	LANDING LOCATION

NOTES & OBSERVATIONS

_____

_____

_____

AIRTIME DURATION		FLIGHT CENTER STAMP	
TODAY			☐ INSTRUCTOR
TO DATE			☐ FLIGHT TUTOR
ALL TIME			☐ FLIGHT BUDDY

SIGNATURE _____

LOCATION							DATE	
PARAGLIDER								
PARAMOTOR							/ /	

LAUNCH TYPE						AIRTIME		
						AIR DISTANCE		

WEATHER CONDITION	☀	☁	❄	⛈	〰	TIME OF YEAR	🌷 ☀ 🍂 ❄

FLIGHT START	🕐		GEAR CHECKLIST	
FLIGHT FINISH			☐ PARAGLIDER	☐ HARNESS
SLOPE GRADIENT	↑ ↓		☐ GOGGLES	☐ HELMET
			☐ RESERVE	☐ GLOVES

LAUNCH LOCATION	LANDING LOCATION

NOTES & OBSERVATIONS

_____

_____

_____

AIRTIME DURATION		FLIGHT CENTER STAMP	
TODAY			☐ INSTRUCTOR
TO DATE			☐ FLIGHT TUTOR
ALL TIME			☐ FLIGHT BUDDY

SIGNATURE

_____

LOCATION		DATE
PARAGLIDER		
PARAMOTOR		/ /

LAUNCH TYPE		AIRTIME	
		AIR DISTANCE	

WEATHER CONDITION	☀ ☁ ❄ ⛈ 🌬	TIME OF YEAR	🌷 ☀ 🍁 ❄

FLIGHT START	🕐	GEAR CHECKLIST	
FLIGHT FINISH		☐ PARAGLIDER	☐ HARNESS
SLOPE GRADIENT	↑ ↓	☐ GOGGLES	☐ HELMET
		☐ RESERVE	☐ GLOVES

LAUNCH LOCATION	LANDING LOCATION

NOTES & OBSERVATIONS

_____

_____

_____

AIRTIME DURATION		FLIGHT CENTER STAMP	
TODAY			☐ INSTRUCTOR
TO DATE			☐ FLIGHT TUTOR
ALL TIME			☐ FLIGHT BUDDY

SIGNATURE

_____

LOCATION		DATE
PARAGLIDER		
PARAMOTOR		/ /

LAUNCH TYPE		AIRTIME	
		AIR DISTANCE	

WEATHER CONDITION	☀ ☁ ❄ ⛈ 💨	TIME OF YEAR	🌷 ☀ 🍁 ❄

FLIGHT START	🕐	GEAR CHECKLIST	
FLIGHT FINISH		☐ PARAGLIDER	☐ HARNESS
SLOPE GRADIENT	↑ ↓	☐ GOGGLES	☐ HELMET
		☐ RESERVE	☐ GLOVES

LAUNCH LOCATION	LANDING LOCATION

NOTES & OBSERVATIONS

_____

_____

_____

AIRTIME DURATION		FLIGHT CENTER STAMP	
TODAY			☐ INSTRUCTOR
TO DATE			☐ FLIGHT TUTOR
ALL TIME			☐ FLIGHT BUDDY

SIGNATURE _____

LOCATION		DATE
PARAGLIDER		
PARAMOTOR		/ /

LAUNCH TYPE		AIRTIME	
		AIR DISTANCE	

WEATHER CONDITION	☀ ☁ ❄ ⛈ 🌬	TIME OF YEAR	🌷 ☀ 🍃 ❄

FLIGHT START	🕐	GEAR CHECKLIST	
FLIGHT FINISH		☐ PARAGLIDER	☐ HARNESS
SLOPE GRADIENT	↑ ↓	☐ GOGGLES	☐ HELMET
		☐ RESERVE	☐ GLOVES

LAUNCH LOCATION	LANDING LOCATION

NOTES & OBSERVATIONS

_____

_____

_____

_____

AIRTIME DURATION		FLIGHT CENTER STAMP	
TODAY			☐ INSTRUCTOR
TO DATE			☐ FLIGHT TUTOR
ALL TIME			☐ FLIGHT BUDDY

SIGNATURE _____

LOCATION		DATE
PARAGLIDER		
PARAMOTOR		/ /

LAUNCH TYPE		AIRTIME	
		AIR DISTANCE	

WEATHER CONDITION	☀ ☁ ❄ ⛈ 🌬	TIME OF YEAR	🌷 ☀ 🍁 ❄

FLIGHT START	🕐	GEAR CHECKLIST	
FLIGHT FINISH		☐ PARAGLIDER	☐ HARNESS
SLOPE GRADIENT	↑ ↓	☐ GOGGLES	☐ HELMET
		☐ RESERVE	☐ GLOVES

LAUNCH LOCATION   LANDING LOCATION

NOTES & OBSERVATIONS

_____

_____

_____

AIRTIME DURATION   FLIGHT CENTER STAMP

TODAY			☐ INSTRUCTOR
TO DATE			☐ FLIGHT TUTOR
ALL TIME			☐ FLIGHT BUDDY

SIGNATURE _____

LOCATION		DATE
PARAGLIDER		
PARAMOTOR		/ /

LAUNCH TYPE		AIRTIME	
		AIR DISTANCE	

WEATHER CONDITION	☀ ☁ ❄ ⛈ 🌬	TIME OF YEAR	🌷 ☀ 🍃 ❄

FLIGHT START	🕐	GEAR CHECKLIST	
FLIGHT FINISH		☐ PARAGLIDER	☐ HARNESS
SLOPE GRADIENT	↑↓	☐ GOGGLES	☐ HELMET
		☐ RESERVE	☐ GLOVES

LAUNCH LOCATION	LANDING LOCATION

NOTES & OBSERVATIONS

_____

_____

_____

AIRTIME DURATION		FLIGHT CENTER STAMP	
TODAY			☐ INSTRUCTOR
TO DATE			☐ FLIGHT TUTOR
ALL TIME			☐ FLIGHT BUDDY

SIGNATURE

_____

LOCATION		DATE
PARAGLIDER		
PARAMOTOR		/ /

LAUNCH TYPE		AIRTIME	
		AIR DISTANCE	

WEATHER CONDITION	☀ ☁ ❄ ⛈ 🌬	TIME OF YEAR	🌷 ☀ 🍁 ❄

FLIGHT START	🕐	GEAR CHECKLIST	
FLIGHT FINISH		☐ PARAGLIDER	☐ HARNESS
SLOPE GRADIENT	↑ ↓	☐ GOGGLES	☐ HELMET
		☐ RESERVE	☐ GLOVES

LAUNCH LOCATION	LANDING LOCATION

NOTES & OBSERVATIONS

_____

_____

_____

AIRTIME DURATION		FLIGHT CENTER STAMP	
TODAY			☐ INSTRUCTOR
TO DATE			☐ FLIGHT TUTOR
ALL TIME			☐ FLIGHT BUDDY

SIGNATURE _____

LOCATION		DATE
PARAGLIDER		
PARAMOTOR		/ /

LAUNCH TYPE		AIRTIME	
		AIR DISTANCE	

WEATHER CONDITION	☀ ☁ ❄ 🌧 💨	TIME OF YEAR	🌷 ☀ 🍃 ❄

FLIGHT START	🕐	GEAR CHECKLIST	
FLIGHT FINISH		☐ PARAGLIDER	☐ HARNESS
SLOPE GRADIENT	↑↓	☐ GOGGLES	☐ HELMET
		☐ RESERVE	☐ GLOVES

LAUNCH LOCATION	LANDING LOCATION

NOTES & OBSERVATIONS

AIRTIME DURATION		FLIGHT CENTER STAMP	
TODAY			☐ INSTRUCTOR
TO DATE			☐ FLIGHT TUTOR
ALL TIME			☐ FLIGHT BUDDY

SIGNATURE

LOCATION		DATE
PARAGLIDER		
PARAMOTOR		/ /

LAUNCH TYPE		AIRTIME	
		AIR DISTANCE	

WEATHER CONDITION	☀ ☁ ❄ ⛈ ≈	TIME OF YEAR	🌷 ☀ 🍃 ❄

FLIGHT START	🕐	GEAR CHECKLIST	
FLIGHT FINISH		☐ PARAGLIDER	☐ HARNESS
SLOPE GRADIENT	↑ ↓	☐ GOGGLES	☐ HELMET
		☐ RESERVE	☐ GLOVES

LAUNCH LOCATION	LANDING LOCATION

NOTES & OBSERVATIONS

_____

_____

_____

AIRTIME DURATION

TODAY	
TO DATE	
ALL TIME	

FLIGHT CENTER STAMP

☐ INSTRUCTOR

☐ FLIGHT TUTOR

☐ FLIGHT BUDDY

SIGNATURE _____

LOCATION		DATE	
PARAGLIDER			
PARAMOTOR		/ /	

LAUNCH TYPE		AIRTIME	
		AIR DISTANCE	

WEATHER CONDITION	☀ ☁ ❄ ⛈ 🌬	TIME OF YEAR	🌷 ☀ 🍃 ❄

FLIGHT START	🕐	GEAR CHECKLIST	
FLIGHT FINISH		☐ PARAGLIDER ☐ HARNESS	
SLOPE GRADIENT	↑↓	☐ GOGGLES ☐ HELMET	
		☐ RESERVE ☐ GLOVES	

LAUNCH LOCATION	LANDING LOCATION

NOTES & OBSERVATIONS

_____

_____

_____

AIRTIME DURATION		FLIGHT CENTER STAMP	
TODAY			☐ INSTRUCTOR
TO DATE			☐ FLIGHT TUTOR
ALL TIME			☐ FLIGHT BUDDY

SIGNATURE

_____

LOCATION		DATE
PARAGLIDER		
PARAMOTOR		/ /

LAUNCH TYPE		AIRTIME	
		AIR DISTANCE	

WEATHER CONDITION	☀ ☁ ❄ ⛈ 🌬	TIME OF YEAR	🌷 ☀ 🍂 ❄

FLIGHT START	🕐		GEAR CHECKLIST	
FLIGHT FINISH			☐ PARAGLIDER	☐ HARNESS
SLOPE GRADIENT	↑ ↓		☐ GOGGLES	☐ HELMET
			☐ RESERVE	☐ GLOVES

LAUNCH LOCATION	LANDING LOCATION

NOTES & OBSERVATIONS

_____

_____

_____

AIRTIME DURATION		FLIGHT CENTER STAMP	
TODAY			☐ INSTRUCTOR
TO DATE			☐ FLIGHT TUTOR
ALL TIME			☐ FLIGHT BUDDY

SIGNATURE
_____

LOCATION		DATE
PARAGLIDER		
PARAMOTOR		/ /

LAUNCH TYPE		AIRTIME	
		AIR DISTANCE	

WEATHER CONDITION	☀ ☁ ❄ ⛈ 🌬	TIME OF YEAR	🌷 ☀ 🍃 ❄

FLIGHT START	🕐	GEAR CHECKLIST	
FLIGHT FINISH		☐ PARAGLIDER	☐ HARNESS
SLOPE GRADIENT	↑ ↓	☐ GOGGLES	☐ HELMET
		☐ RESERVE	☐ GLOVES

LAUNCH LOCATION	LANDING LOCATION

NOTES & OBSERVATIONS

AIRTIME DURATION		FLIGHT CENTER STAMP	
TODAY			☐ INSTRUCTOR
TO DATE			☐ FLIGHT TUTOR
ALL TIME			☐ FLIGHT BUDDY

SIGNATURE

LOCATION		DATE
PARAGLIDER		
PARAMOTOR		/ /

LAUNCH TYPE		AIRTIME	
		AIR DISTANCE	

WEATHER CONDITION	☀ ☁ ❄ ⛈ 🌬	TIME OF YEAR	🌷 ☀ 🍃 ❄

FLIGHT START	🕐	GEAR CHECKLIST	
FLIGHT FINISH		☐ PARAGLIDER	☐ HARNESS
SLOPE GRADIENT	↑ ↓	☐ GOGGLES	☐ HELMET
		☐ RESERVE	☐ GLOVES

LAUNCH LOCATION	LANDING LOCATION

NOTES & OBSERVATIONS

_____

_____

_____

AIRTIME DURATION		FLIGHT CENTER STAMP	
TODAY			☐ INSTRUCTOR
TO DATE			☐ FLIGHT TUTOR
ALL TIME			☐ FLIGHT BUDDY

SIGNATURE _____

LOCATION		DATE
PARAGLIDER		
PARAMOTOR		/ /

LAUNCH TYPE		AIRTIME	
		AIR DISTANCE	

WEATHER CONDITION	☀ ☁ ❄ ⛈ 🌬	TIME OF YEAR	🌷 ☀ 🍃 ❄

FLIGHT START	🕐	GEAR CHECKLIST	
FLIGHT FINISH		☐ PARAGLIDER	☐ HARNESS
SLOPE GRADIENT	↑ ↓	☐ GOGGLES	☐ HELMET
		☐ RESERVE	☐ GLOVES

LAUNCH LOCATION	LANDING LOCATION

NOTES & OBSERVATIONS

_____

_____

_____

AIRTIME DURATION		FLIGHT CENTER STAMP	
TODAY			☐ INSTRUCTOR
TO DATE			☐ FLIGHT TUTOR
ALL TIME			☐ FLIGHT BUDDY

SIGNATURE

_____

LOCATION		DATE
PARAGLIDER		
PARAMOTOR		/ /

LAUNCH TYPE		AIRTIME	
		AIR DISTANCE	

WEATHER CONDITION	☀ ☁ ❄ ⛈ 〜	TIME OF YEAR	🌷 ☀ 🍃 ❄

FLIGHT START	🕐	GEAR CHECKLIST	
FLIGHT FINISH		☐ PARAGLIDER	☐ HARNESS
SLOPE GRADIENT	↑ ↓	☐ GOGGLES	☐ HELMET
		☐ RESERVE	☐ GLOVES

LAUNCH LOCATION	LANDING LOCATION

NOTES & OBSERVATIONS

_____

_____

_____

AIRTIME DURATION		FLIGHT CENTER STAMP	
TODAY			☐ INSTRUCTOR
TO DATE			☐ FLIGHT TUTOR
ALL TIME			☐ FLIGHT BUDDY

SIGNATURE _____

LOCATION		DATE
PARAGLIDER		
PARAMOTOR		/ /

LAUNCH TYPE		AIRTIME	
		AIR DISTANCE	

WEATHER CONDITION	☀ ☁ ❄ ⛈ 🌬	TIME OF YEAR	🌷 ☀ 🍃 ❄

FLIGHT START	🕐	GEAR CHECKLIST	
FLIGHT FINISH		☐ PARAGLIDER ☐ HARNESS	
SLOPE GRADIENT	↑↓	☐ GOGGLES ☐ HELMET	
		☐ RESERVE ☐ GLOVES	

LAUNCH LOCATION	LANDING LOCATION

NOTES & OBSERVATIONS

_____

_____

_____

_____

AIRTIME DURATION		FLIGHT CENTER STAMP	
TODAY			☐ INSTRUCTOR
TO DATE			☐ FLIGHT TUTOR
ALL TIME			☐ FLIGHT BUDDY

SIGNATURE

_____

LOCATION		DATE
PARAGLIDER		
PARAMOTOR		/ /

LAUNCH TYPE		AIRTIME	
		AIR DISTANCE	

WEATHER CONDITION	☀ ☁ ❄ ⛈ 💨	TIME OF YEAR	🌷 ☀ 🍁 ❄

FLIGHT START	🕐	GEAR CHECKLIST	
FLIGHT FINISH		☐ PARAGLIDER	☐ HARNESS
SLOPE GRADIENT	↑ ↓	☐ GOGGLES	☐ HELMET
		☐ RESERVE	☐ GLOVES

LAUNCH LOCATION	LANDING LOCATION

NOTES & OBSERVATIONS

_____

_____

_____

AIRTIME DURATION

		FLIGHT CENTER STAMP	
TODAY			☐ INSTRUCTOR
TO DATE			☐ FLIGHT TUTOR
ALL TIME			☐ FLIGHT BUDDY

SIGNATURE _____

LOCATION		DATE
PARAGLIDER		
PARAMOTOR		/ /

LAUNCH TYPE		AIRTIME	
		AIR DISTANCE	

WEATHER CONDITION	☀ ☁ ❄ ⛈ 〜	TIME OF YEAR	🌷 ☀ 🍃 ❄

FLIGHT START	🕐	GEAR CHECKLIST	
FLIGHT FINISH		☐ PARAGLIDER	☐ HARNESS
SLOPE GRADIENT	↑ ↓	☐ GOGGLES	☐ HELMET
		☐ RESERVE	☐ GLOVES

LAUNCH LOCATION	LANDING LOCATION

NOTES & OBSERVATIONS

_____

_____

_____

_____

AIRTIME DURATION		FLIGHT CENTER STAMP	
TODAY			☐ INSTRUCTOR
TO DATE			☐ FLIGHT TUTOR
ALL TIME			☐ FLIGHT BUDDY

SIGNATURE _____

LOCATION		DATE
PARAGLIDER		
PARAMOTOR		/ /

LAUNCH TYPE		AIRTIME	
		AIR DISTANCE	

WEATHER CONDITION	☀ ☁ ❄ ⛈ 🌬	TIME OF YEAR	🌷 ☀ 🍂 ❄

FLIGHT START	🕐	GEAR CHECKLIST	
FLIGHT FINISH		☐ PARAGLIDER	☐ HARNESS
SLOPE GRADIENT	↑ ↓	☐ GOGGLES	☐ HELMET
		☐ RESERVE	☐ GLOVES

LAUNCH LOCATION	LANDING LOCATION

NOTES & OBSERVATIONS

_____

_____

_____

AIRTIME DURATION		FLIGHT CENTER STAMP	
TODAY			☐ INSTRUCTOR
TO DATE			☐ FLIGHT TUTOR
ALL TIME			☐ FLIGHT BUDDY

SIGNATURE _____

LOCATION		DATE
PARAGLIDER		
PARAMOTOR		/ /

LAUNCH TYPE		AIRTIME	
		AIR DISTANCE	

WEATHER CONDITION	☀ ☁ ❄ 🌦 💨	TIME OF YEAR	🌷 ☀ 🍃 ❄

FLIGHT START	🕐	GEAR CHECKLIST	
FLIGHT FINISH		☐ PARAGLIDER	☐ HARNESS
SLOPE GRADIENT	↑↓	☐ GOGGLES	☐ HELMET
		☐ RESERVE	☐ GLOVES

LAUNCH LOCATION	LANDING LOCATION

NOTES & OBSERVATIONS

_____

_____

_____

_____

AIRTIME DURATION		FLIGHT CENTER STAMP	
TODAY			☐ INSTRUCTOR
TO DATE			☐ FLIGHT TUTOR
ALL TIME			☐ FLIGHT BUDDY

SIGNATURE

_____

LOCATION		DATE
PARAGLIDER		
PARAMOTOR		/ /

LAUNCH TYPE		AIRTIME	
		AIR DISTANCE	

WEATHER CONDITION	☀ ☁ ❄ ⛈ 🌬	TIME OF YEAR	🌷 ☀ 🍂 ❄

FLIGHT START	🕐	GEAR CHECKLIST	
FLIGHT FINISH		☐ PARAGLIDER	☐ HARNESS
SLOPE GRADIENT	↑ ↓	☐ GOGGLES	☐ HELMET
		☐ RESERVE	☐ GLOVES

LAUNCH LOCATION	LANDING LOCATION

NOTES & OBSERVATIONS

_____

_____

_____

AIRTIME DURATION		FLIGHT CENTER STAMP	
TODAY			☐ INSTRUCTOR
TO DATE			☐ FLIGHT TUTOR
ALL TIME			☐ FLIGHT BUDDY

SIGNATURE

_____

LOCATION		DATE
PARAGLIDER		
PARAMOTOR		/ /

LAUNCH TYPE		AIRTIME	
		AIR DISTANCE	

WEATHER CONDITION	☀ ☁ ❄ ⛈ 💨	TIME OF YEAR	🌷 ☀ 🍃 ❄

FLIGHT START	🕐	GEAR CHECKLIST	
FLIGHT FINISH		☐ PARAGLIDER ☐ HARNESS	
SLOPE GRADIENT	↑ ↓	☐ GOGGLES ☐ HELMET	
		☐ RESERVE ☐ GLOVES	

LAUNCH LOCATION	LANDING LOCATION

NOTES & OBSERVATIONS

_____

_____

_____

AIRTIME DURATION		FLIGHT CENTER STAMP	
TODAY			☐ INSTRUCTOR
TO DATE			☐ FLIGHT TUTOR
ALL TIME			☐ FLIGHT BUDDY

SIGNATURE

_____

LOCATION		DATE
PARAGLIDER		
PARAMOTOR		/ /

LAUNCH TYPE		AIRTIME	
		AIR DISTANCE	

WEATHER CONDITION	☀ ☁ ❄ ⛈ 🌬	TIME OF YEAR	🌷 ☀ 🍃 ❄

FLIGHT START	🕐	GEAR CHECKLIST	
FLIGHT FINISH		☐ PARAGLIDER	☐ HARNESS
SLOPE GRADIENT	↑↓	☐ GOGGLES	☐ HELMET
		☐ RESERVE	☐ GLOVES

LAUNCH LOCATION	LANDING LOCATION

NOTES & OBSERVATIONS

_____

_____

_____

AIRTIME DURATION		FLIGHT CENTER STAMP	
TODAY			☐ INSTRUCTOR
TO DATE			☐ FLIGHT TUTOR
ALL TIME			☐ FLIGHT BUDDY

SIGNATURE _____

LOCATION		DATE
PARAGLIDER		
PARAMOTOR		/ /

LAUNCH TYPE		AIRTIME	
		AIR DISTANCE	

WEATHER CONDITION	☀ ☁ ❄ ⚡ 🌬	TIME OF YEAR	🌷 ☀ 🍃 ❄

FLIGHT START	🕐	GEAR CHECKLIST	
FLIGHT FINISH		☐ PARAGLIDER ☐ HARNESS	
SLOPE GRADIENT	↑↓	☐ GOGGLES ☐ HELMET	
		☐ RESERVE ☐ GLOVES	

LAUNCH LOCATION	LANDING LOCATION

NOTES & OBSERVATIONS

AIRTIME DURATION		FLIGHT CENTER STAMP	
TODAY			☐ INSTRUCTOR
TO DATE			☐ FLIGHT TUTOR
ALL TIME			☐ FLIGHT BUDDY

SIGNATURE

LOCATION		DATE
PARAGLIDER		
PARAMOTOR		/ /

LAUNCH TYPE		AIRTIME	
		AIR DISTANCE	

WEATHER CONDITION	☀ ☁ ❄ ⛈ 🌬	TIME OF YEAR	🌷 ☀ 🍁 ❄

FLIGHT START	🕐	GEAR CHECKLIST	
FLIGHT FINISH		☐ PARAGLIDER	☐ HARNESS
SLOPE GRADIENT	↑↓	☐ GOGGLES	☐ HELMET
		☐ RESERVE	☐ GLOVES

LAUNCH LOCATION

LANDING LOCATION

NOTES & OBSERVATIONS

_____

_____

_____

AIRTIME DURATION		FLIGHT CENTER STAMP	
TODAY			☐ INSTRUCTOR
TO DATE			☐ FLIGHT TUTOR
ALL TIME			☐ FLIGHT BUDDY

SIGNATURE

_____

LOCATION		DATE
PARAGLIDER		
PARAMOTOR		/ /

LAUNCH TYPE		AIRTIME	
		AIR DISTANCE	

WEATHER CONDITION	☀ ☁ ❄ ⛈ 🌬	TIME OF YEAR	🌷 ☀ 🍃 ❄

FLIGHT START	🕐	GEAR CHECKLIST	
FLIGHT FINISH		☐ PARAGLIDER	☐ HARNESS
SLOPE GRADIENT	↑ ↓	☐ GOGGLES	☐ HELMET
		☐ RESERVE	☐ GLOVES

LAUNCH LOCATION	LANDING LOCATION

NOTES & OBSERVATIONS

_____

_____

AIRTIME DURATION		FLIGHT CENTER STAMP	
TODAY			☐ INSTRUCTOR
TO DATE			☐ FLIGHT TUTOR
ALL TIME			☐ FLIGHT BUDDY

SIGNATURE

_____

LOCATION		DATE
PARAGLIDER		
PARAMOTOR		/ /

LAUNCH TYPE		AIRTIME	
		AIR DISTANCE	

WEATHER CONDITION	☀ ☔ ❄ ⛈ 🌬	TIME OF YEAR	🌷 ☀ 🍁 ❄

FLIGHT START	🕐	GEAR CHECKLIST	
FLIGHT FINISH		☐ PARAGLIDER	☐ HARNESS
SLOPE GRADIENT	↑ ↓	☐ GOGGLES	☐ HELMET
		☐ RESERVE	☐ GLOVES

LAUNCH LOCATION	LANDING LOCATION

NOTES & OBSERVATIONS

_____

_____

_____

AIRTIME DURATION

AIRTIME DURATION		FLIGHT CENTER STAMP	
TODAY			☐ INSTRUCTOR
TO DATE			☐ FLIGHT TUTOR
ALL TIME			☐ FLIGHT BUDDY

SIGNATURE

_____

LOCATION		DATE
PARAGLIDER		
PARAMOTOR		/ /

LAUNCH TYPE		AIRTIME	
		AIR DISTANCE	

WEATHER CONDITION	☀ ☁ ❄ ⛈ 🌬	TIME OF YEAR	🌷 ☀ 🍂 ❄

FLIGHT START	🕐	GEAR CHECKLIST	
FLIGHT FINISH		☐ PARAGLIDER	☐ HARNESS
SLOPE GRADIENT	↑↓	☐ GOGGLES	☐ HELMET
		☐ RESERVE	☐ GLOVES

LAUNCH LOCATION	LANDING LOCATION

NOTES & OBSERVATIONS

_____

_____

_____

AIRTIME DURATION		FLIGHT CENTER STAMP	
TODAY			☐ INSTRUCTOR
TO DATE			☐ FLIGHT TUTOR
ALL TIME			☐ FLIGHT BUDDY

SIGNATURE

_____

LOCATION		DATE	
PARAGLIDER			
PARAMOTOR		/ /	

LAUNCH TYPE		AIRTIME	
		AIR DISTANCE	

WEATHER CONDITION	☀ ☁ ❄ ⛈ 🌬	TIME OF YEAR	🌷 ☀ 🍁 ❄

FLIGHT START	🕐	GEAR CHECKLIST	
FLIGHT FINISH		☐ PARAGLIDER	☐ HARNESS
SLOPE GRADIENT	↑ ↓	☐ GOGGLES	☐ HELMET
		☐ RESERVE	☐ GLOVES

LAUNCH LOCATION	LANDING LOCATION

NOTES & OBSERVATIONS

_____

_____

_____

AIRTIME DURATION		FLIGHT CENTER STAMP	
TODAY			☐ INSTRUCTOR
TO DATE			☐ FLIGHT TUTOR
ALL TIME			☐ FLIGHT BUDDY

SIGNATURE

_____

LOCATION		DATE
PARAGLIDER		
PARAMOTOR		/ /

LAUNCH TYPE		AIRTIME	
		AIR DISTANCE	

WEATHER CONDITION	☀ ☁ ❄ ⛈ 🌬	TIME OF YEAR	🌷 ☀ 🍃 ❄

FLIGHT START	🕐	GEAR CHECKLIST	
FLIGHT FINISH		☐ PARAGLIDER	☐ HARNESS
SLOPE GRADIENT	↑ ↓	☐ GOGGLES	☐ HELMET
		☐ RESERVE	☐ GLOVES

LAUNCH LOCATION	LANDING LOCATION

NOTES & OBSERVATIONS

_____

_____

_____

AIRTIME DURATION		FLIGHT CENTER STAMP	
TODAY			☐ INSTRUCTOR
TO DATE			☐ FLIGHT TUTOR
ALL TIME			☐ FLIGHT BUDDY

SIGNATURE _____

LOCATION		DATE
PARAGLIDER		
PARAMOTOR		/ /

LAUNCH TYPE		AIRTIME	
		AIR DISTANCE	

WEATHER CONDITION	☀ ☁ ❄ ⛈ 🌬	TIME OF YEAR	🌷 ☀ 🍃 ❄

FLIGHT START	🕐	GEAR CHECKLIST	
FLIGHT FINISH		☐ PARAGLIDER	☐ HARNESS
SLOPE GRADIENT	↑ ↓	☐ GOGGLES	☐ HELMET
		☐ RESERVE	☐ GLOVES

LAUNCH LOCATION	LANDING LOCATION

NOTES & OBSERVATIONS

_____

_____

_____

AIRTIME DURATION		FLIGHT CENTER STAMP	
TODAY			☐ INSTRUCTOR
TO DATE			☐ FLIGHT TUTOR
ALL TIME			☐ FLIGHT BUDDY

SIGNATURE

_____

LOCATION		DATE
PARAGLIDER		
PARAMOTOR		/ /

LAUNCH TYPE		AIRTIME	
		AIR DISTANCE	

WEATHER CONDITION	☀ ☁ ❄ ⛈ 🌬	TIME OF YEAR	🌷 ☀ 🍃 ❄

FLIGHT START	🕐	GEAR CHECKLIST	
FLIGHT FINISH		☐ PARAGLIDER	☐ HARNESS
SLOPE GRADIENT	↑ ↓	☐ GOGGLES	☐ HELMET
		☐ RESERVE	☐ GLOVES

LAUNCH LOCATION	LANDING LOCATION

NOTES & OBSERVATIONS

_____

_____

_____

AIRTIME DURATION		FLIGHT CENTER STAMP	
TODAY			☐ INSTRUCTOR
TO DATE			☐ FLIGHT TUTOR
ALL TIME			☐ FLIGHT BUDDY

SIGNATURE _____

LOCATION		DATE
PARAGLIDER		
PARAMOTOR		/ /

LAUNCH TYPE		AIRTIME	
		AIR DISTANCE	

WEATHER CONDITION	☀ 🌧 ❄ ⛈ 🌬	TIME OF YEAR	🌷 ☀ 🍃 ❄

FLIGHT START	🕐	GEAR CHECKLIST	
FLIGHT FINISH		☐ PARAGLIDER	☐ HARNESS
SLOPE GRADIENT	↑ ↓	☐ GOGGLES	☐ HELMET
		☐ RESERVE	☐ GLOVES

LAUNCH LOCATION	LANDING LOCATION

NOTES & OBSERVATIONS

_____

_____

_____

AIRTIME DURATION		FLIGHT CENTER STAMP	
TODAY			☐ INSTRUCTOR
TO DATE			☐ FLIGHT TUTOR
ALL TIME			☐ FLIGHT BUDDY

SIGNATURE

_____

LOCATION		DATE
PARAGLIDER		
PARAMOTOR		/ /

LAUNCH TYPE		AIRTIME	
		AIR DISTANCE	

WEATHER CONDITION	☀ ☁ ❄ ⛈ 🌬	TIME OF YEAR	🌷 ☀ 🍃 ❄

FLIGHT START	🕐		GEAR CHECKLIST	
FLIGHT FINISH			☐ PARAGLIDER	☐ HARNESS
SLOPE GRADIENT	↑ ↓		☐ GOGGLES	☐ HELMET
			☐ RESERVE	☐ GLOVES

LAUNCH LOCATION	LANDING LOCATION

NOTES & OBSERVATIONS

_____

_____

_____

AIRTIME DURATION		FLIGHT CENTER STAMP	
TODAY			☐ INSTRUCTOR
TO DATE			☐ FLIGHT TUTOR
ALL TIME			☐ FLIGHT BUDDY

SIGNATURE

_____

LOCATION		DATE
PARAGLIDER		
PARAMOTOR		/ /

LAUNCH TYPE		AIRTIME	
		AIR DISTANCE	

WEATHER CONDITION	☀ ☁ ❄ ⛈ 🌬	TIME OF YEAR	🌷 ☀ 🍂 ❄

FLIGHT START	🕐	GEAR CHECKLIST	
FLIGHT FINISH		☐ PARAGLIDER	☐ HARNESS
SLOPE GRADIENT	↑ ↓	☐ GOGGLES	☐ HELMET
		☐ RESERVE	☐ GLOVES

LAUNCH LOCATION	LANDING LOCATION

NOTES & OBSERVATIONS

_____

_____

_____

AIRTIME DURATION		FLIGHT CENTER STAMP	
TODAY			☐ INSTRUCTOR
TO DATE			☐ FLIGHT TUTOR
ALL TIME			☐ FLIGHT BUDDY

SIGNATURE _____

LOCATION		DATE
PARAGLIDER		
PARAMOTOR		/ /

LAUNCH TYPE		AIRTIME	
		AIR DISTANCE	

WEATHER CONDITION	☀ ☁ ❄ ⛈ 🌬	TIME OF YEAR	🌷 ☀ 🍃 ❄

FLIGHT START	🕐	GEAR CHECKLIST	
FLIGHT FINISH		☐ PARAGLIDER	☐ HARNESS
SLOPE GRADIENT	↑ ↓	☐ GOGGLES	☐ HELMET
		☐ RESERVE	☐ GLOVES

LAUNCH LOCATION	LANDING LOCATION

NOTES & OBSERVATIONS

_____

_____

_____

AIRTIME DURATION		FLIGHT CENTER STAMP	
TODAY			☐ INSTRUCTOR
TO DATE			☐ FLIGHT TUTOR
ALL TIME			☐ FLIGHT BUDDY

SIGNATURE

_____

LOCATION		DATE	
PARAGLIDER			
PARAMOTOR		/ /	

LAUNCH TYPE		AIRTIME	
		AIR DISTANCE	

WEATHER CONDITION	☀ ☔ ❄ ⛈ 🌬	TIME OF YEAR	🌷 ☀ 🍁 ❄

FLIGHT START	🕐	GEAR CHECKLIST	
FLIGHT FINISH		☐ PARAGLIDER	☐ HARNESS
SLOPE GRADIENT	↑ ↓	☐ GOGGLES	☐ HELMET
		☐ RESERVE	☐ GLOVES

LAUNCH LOCATION	LANDING LOCATION

NOTES & OBSERVATIONS

_____

_____

_____

AIRTIME DURATION		FLIGHT CENTER STAMP	
TODAY			☐ INSTRUCTOR
TO DATE			☐ FLIGHT TUTOR
ALL TIME			☐ FLIGHT BUDDY

SIGNATURE

_____

LOCATION		DATE
PARAGLIDER		
PARAMOTOR		/ /

LAUNCH TYPE		AIRTIME	
		AIR DISTANCE	

WEATHER CONDITION	☀ ☁ ❄ ⛈ 🌬	TIME OF YEAR	🌷 ☀ 🍃 ❄

FLIGHT START	🕐	GEAR CHECKLIST	
FLIGHT FINISH		☐ PARAGLIDER	☐ HARNESS
SLOPE GRADIENT	↑ ↓	☐ GOGGLES	☐ HELMET
		☐ RESERVE	☐ GLOVES

LAUNCH LOCATION	LANDING LOCATION

NOTES & OBSERVATIONS

AIRTIME DURATION		FLIGHT CENTER STAMP	
TODAY			☐ INSTRUCTOR
TO DATE			☐ FLIGHT TUTOR
ALL TIME			☐ FLIGHT BUDDY

SIGNATURE

LOCATION		DATE	
PARAGLIDER			
PARAMOTOR		/ /	

LAUNCH TYPE		AIRTIME	
		AIR DISTANCE	

WEATHER CONDITION	☀ 🌧 ❄ ⛈ 💨	TIME OF YEAR	🌷 ☀ 🍁 ❄

FLIGHT START	🕐	GEAR CHECKLIST	
FLIGHT FINISH		☐ PARAGLIDER	☐ HARNESS
SLOPE GRADIENT	↑ ↓	☐ GOGGLES	☐ HELMET
		☐ RESERVE	☐ GLOVES

LAUNCH LOCATION	LANDING LOCATION

NOTES & OBSERVATIONS

_____

_____

_____

AIRTIME DURATION		FLIGHT CENTER STAMP	
TODAY			☐ INSTRUCTOR
TO DATE			☐ FLIGHT TUTOR
ALL TIME			☐ FLIGHT BUDDY

SIGNATURE

_____

LOCATION		DATE
PARAGLIDER		
PARAMOTOR		/ /

LAUNCH TYPE		AIRTIME	
		AIR DISTANCE	

WEATHER CONDITION	☀ ☁ ❄ ⛈ 🌬	TIME OF YEAR	🌷 ☀ 🍃 ❄

FLIGHT START	🕐	GEAR CHECKLIST	
FLIGHT FINISH		☐ PARAGLIDER	☐ HARNESS
SLOPE GRADIENT	↑↓	☐ GOGGLES	☐ HELMET
		☐ RESERVE	☐ GLOVES

LAUNCH LOCATION	LANDING LOCATION

NOTES & OBSERVATIONS

_____

_____

_____

AIRTIME DURATION		FLIGHT CENTER STAMP	
TODAY			☐ INSTRUCTOR
TO DATE			☐ FLIGHT TUTOR
ALL TIME			☐ FLIGHT BUDDY

SIGNATURE

_____

LOCATION		DATE
PARAGLIDER		
PARAMOTOR		/ /

LAUNCH TYPE		AIRTIME	
		AIR DISTANCE	

WEATHER CONDITION	☀ ☁ ❄ ⛈ 🌬	TIME OF YEAR	🌷 ☀ 🍁 ❄

FLIGHT START	🕐	GEAR CHECKLIST	
FLIGHT FINISH		☐ PARAGLIDER	☐ HARNESS
SLOPE GRADIENT	↑ ↓	☐ GOGGLES	☐ HELMET
		☐ RESERVE	☐ GLOVES

LAUNCH LOCATION	LANDING LOCATION

NOTES & OBSERVATIONS

_____

_____

_____

AIRTIME DURATION		FLIGHT CENTER STAMP	
TODAY			☐ INSTRUCTOR
TO DATE			☐ FLIGHT TUTOR
ALL TIME			☐ FLIGHT BUDDY

SIGNATURE

_____

LOCATION		DATE
PARAGLIDER		
PARAMOTOR		/ /

LAUNCH TYPE		AIRTIME	
		AIR DISTANCE	

WEATHER CONDITION	☀ ☁ ❄ ⚡ 🌬	TIME OF YEAR	🌷 ☀ 🍁 ❄

FLIGHT START	🕐		GEAR CHECKLIST	
FLIGHT FINISH			☐ PARAGLIDER	☐ HARNESS
SLOPE GRADIENT	↑ ↓		☐ GOGGLES	☐ HELMET
			☐ RESERVE	☐ GLOVES

LAUNCH LOCATION	LANDING LOCATION

NOTES & OBSERVATIONS

_____

_____

_____

AIRTIME DURATION		FLIGHT CENTER STAMP
TODAY		☐ INSTRUCTOR
TO DATE		☐ FLIGHT TUTOR
ALL TIME		☐ FLIGHT BUDDY

SIGNATURE _____

LOCATION		DATE
PARAGLIDER		
PARAMOTOR		/ /

LAUNCH TYPE		AIRTIME	
		AIR DISTANCE	

WEATHER CONDITION	☀ 🌧 ❄ ⛈ 🌬	TIME OF YEAR	🌷 ☀ 🍂 ❄

FLIGHT START	🕐	GEAR CHECKLIST	
FLIGHT FINISH		☐ PARAGLIDER	☐ HARNESS
SLOPE GRADIENT	↑ ↓	☐ GOGGLES	☐ HELMET
		☐ RESERVE	☐ GLOVES

LAUNCH LOCATION	LANDING LOCATION

NOTES & OBSERVATIONS

_____

_____

_____

AIRTIME DURATION		FLIGHT CENTER STAMP	
TODAY			☐ INSTRUCTOR
TO DATE			☐ FLIGHT TUTOR
ALL TIME			☐ FLIGHT BUDDY

SIGNATURE

_____

LOCATION		DATE
PARAGLIDER		
PARAMOTOR		/ /

LAUNCH TYPE		AIRTIME	
		AIR DISTANCE	

WEATHER CONDITION	☀ ☁ ❄ ⛈ 🌬	TIME OF YEAR	🌷 ☀ 🍃 ❄

FLIGHT START	🕐	GEAR CHECKLIST	
FLIGHT FINISH		☐ PARAGLIDER ☐ HARNESS	
SLOPE GRADIENT	↑↓	☐ GOGGLES ☐ HELMET	
		☐ RESERVE ☐ GLOVES	

LAUNCH LOCATION	LANDING LOCATION

NOTES & OBSERVATIONS

_____

_____

_____

AIRTIME DURATION		FLIGHT CENTER STAMP	
TODAY			☐ INSTRUCTOR
TO DATE			☐ FLIGHT TUTOR
ALL TIME			☐ FLIGHT BUDDY

SIGNATURE

_____

LOCATION		DATE
PARAGLIDER		
PARAMOTOR		/ /

LAUNCH TYPE		AIRTIME	
		AIR DISTANCE	

WEATHER CONDITION	☀ 🌧 ❄ ⛈ 🌬	TIME OF YEAR	🌷 ☀ 🍂 ❄

FLIGHT START	🕐	GEAR CHECKLIST	
FLIGHT FINISH		☐ PARAGLIDER	☐ HARNESS
SLOPE GRADIENT	↑↓	☐ GOGGLES	☐ HELMET
		☐ RESERVE	☐ GLOVES

LAUNCH LOCATION	LANDING LOCATION

NOTES & OBSERVATIONS

_____

_____

_____

AIRTIME DURATION		FLIGHT CENTER STAMP	
TODAY			☐ INSTRUCTOR
TO DATE			☐ FLIGHT TUTOR
ALL TIME			☐ FLIGHT BUDDY

SIGNATURE

_____

LOCATION		DATE
PARAGLIDER		
PARAMOTOR		/ /

LAUNCH TYPE		AIRTIME	
		AIR DISTANCE	

WEATHER CONDITION	☀ ☁ ❄ ⛈ 🌬	TIME OF YEAR	🌷 ☀ 🍃 ❄

FLIGHT START	🕐	GEAR CHECKLIST	
FLIGHT FINISH		☐ PARAGLIDER	☐ HARNESS
SLOPE GRADIENT	↕	☐ GOGGLES	☐ HELMET
		☐ RESERVE	☐ GLOVES

LAUNCH LOCATION	LANDING LOCATION

NOTES & OBSERVATIONS

_____

_____

_____

AIRTIME DURATION		FLIGHT CENTER STAMP	
TODAY			☐ INSTRUCTOR
TO DATE			☐ FLIGHT TUTOR
ALL TIME			☐ FLIGHT BUDDY

SIGNATURE

_____

LOCATION		DATE
PARAGLIDER		
PARAMOTOR		/ /

LAUNCH TYPE		AIRTIME	
		AIR DISTANCE	

WEATHER CONDITION	☀ ☁ ❄ ⛈ 🌬	TIME OF YEAR	🌷 ☀ 🍃 ❄

FLIGHT START	🕐	GEAR CHECKLIST	
FLIGHT FINISH		☐ PARAGLIDER	☐ HARNESS
SLOPE GRADIENT	↑↓	☐ GOGGLES	☐ HELMET
		☐ RESERVE	☐ GLOVES

LAUNCH LOCATION	LANDING LOCATION

NOTES & OBSERVATIONS

_____

_____

_____

AIRTIME DURATION		FLIGHT CENTER STAMP	
TODAY			☐ INSTRUCTOR
TO DATE			☐ FLIGHT TUTOR
ALL TIME			☐ FLIGHT BUDDY

SIGNATURE

_____

LOCATION		DATE
PARAGLIDER		
PARAMOTOR		/ /

LAUNCH TYPE		AIRTIME	
		AIR DISTANCE	

WEATHER CONDITION	☀ ☁ ❄ ⚡ 💨	TIME OF YEAR	🌷 ☀ 🍃 ❄

FLIGHT START	🕐	GEAR CHECKLIST	
FLIGHT FINISH		☐ PARAGLIDER	☐ HARNESS
SLOPE GRADIENT	↑ ↓	☐ GOGGLES	☐ HELMET
		☐ RESERVE	☐ GLOVES

LAUNCH LOCATION	LANDING LOCATION

NOTES & OBSERVATIONS

_____

_____

_____

AIRTIME DURATION		FLIGHT CENTER STAMP	
TODAY			☐ INSTRUCTOR
TO DATE			☐ FLIGHT TUTOR
ALL TIME			☐ FLIGHT BUDDY

SIGNATURE _____

LOCATION		DATE
PARAGLIDER		
PARAMOTOR		/ /

LAUNCH TYPE		AIRTIME	
		AIR DISTANCE	

WEATHER CONDITION	☀ ☁ ❄ ⛈ 💨	TIME OF YEAR	🌷 ☀ 🍂 ❄

FLIGHT START	🕐		GEAR CHECKLIST	
FLIGHT FINISH			☐ PARAGLIDER	☐ HARNESS
SLOPE GRADIENT	↑ ↓		☐ GOGGLES	☐ HELMET
			☐ RESERVE	☐ GLOVES

LAUNCH LOCATION	LANDING LOCATION

NOTES & OBSERVATIONS

_____

_____

_____

AIRTIME DURATION		FLIGHT CENTER STAMP	
TODAY			☐ INSTRUCTOR
TO DATE			☐ FLIGHT TUTOR
ALL TIME			☐ FLIGHT BUDDY

SIGNATURE

_____

LOCATION		DATE
PARAGLIDER		
PARAMOTOR		/ /

LAUNCH TYPE		AIRTIME	
		AIR DISTANCE	

WEATHER CONDITION	☀ ☁ ❄ ⚡ 🌬	TIME OF YEAR	🌷 ☀ 🍂 ❄

FLIGHT START	🕐	GEAR CHECKLIST	
FLIGHT FINISH		☐ PARAGLIDER	☐ HARNESS
SLOPE GRADIENT	↑ ↓	☐ GOGGLES	☐ HELMET
		☐ RESERVE	☐ GLOVES

LAUNCH LOCATION	LANDING LOCATION

NOTES & OBSERVATIONS

AIRTIME DURATION		FLIGHT CENTER STAMP	
TODAY			☐ INSTRUCTOR
TO DATE			☐ FLIGHT TUTOR
ALL TIME			☐ FLIGHT BUDDY

SIGNATURE

LOCATION		DATE	
PARAGLIDER			
PARAMOTOR		/ /	

LAUNCH TYPE		AIRTIME	
		AIR DISTANCE	

WEATHER CONDITION	☀ ☔ ❄ ⛈ 💨	TIME OF YEAR	🌷 ☀ 🍂 ❄

FLIGHT START	🕐	GEAR CHECKLIST	
FLIGHT FINISH		☐ PARAGLIDER	☐ HARNESS
SLOPE GRADIENT	↑ ↓	☐ GOGGLES	☐ HELMET
		☐ RESERVE	☐ GLOVES

LAUNCH LOCATION	LANDING LOCATION

NOTES & OBSERVATIONS

_____

_____

_____

AIRTIME DURATION		FLIGHT CENTER STAMP	
TODAY			☐ INSTRUCTOR
TO DATE			☐ FLIGHT TUTOR
ALL TIME			☐ FLIGHT BUDDY

SIGNATURE

_____

LOCATION		DATE
PARAGLIDER		
PARAMOTOR		/ /

LAUNCH TYPE		AIRTIME	
		AIR DISTANCE	

WEATHER CONDITION	☀ ☁ ❄ ⚡ 🌬	TIME OF YEAR	🌷 ☀ 🍃 ❄

FLIGHT START	🕐	GEAR CHECKLIST	
FLIGHT FINISH		☐ PARAGLIDER	☐ HARNESS
SLOPE GRADIENT	↕	☐ GOGGLES	☐ HELMET
		☐ RESERVE	☐ GLOVES

LAUNCH LOCATION	LANDING LOCATION

NOTES & OBSERVATIONS

_____

_____

_____

AIRTIME DURATION		FLIGHT CENTER STAMP	
TODAY			☐ INSTRUCTOR
TO DATE			☐ FLIGHT TUTOR
ALL TIME			☐ FLIGHT BUDDY

SIGNATURE _____

LOCATION		DATE	
PARAGLIDER			
PARAMOTOR		/ /	

LAUNCH TYPE		AIRTIME	
		AIR DISTANCE	

WEATHER CONDITION	☀ ☁ ❄ ⛈ 🌬	TIME OF YEAR	🌷 ☀ 🍃 ❄

FLIGHT START	🕐	GEAR CHECKLIST	
FLIGHT FINISH		☐ PARAGLIDER	☐ HARNESS
SLOPE GRADIENT	↑ ↓	☐ GOGGLES	☐ HELMET
		☐ RESERVE	☐ GLOVES

LAUNCH LOCATION	LANDING LOCATION

NOTES & OBSERVATIONS

_____

_____

_____

AIRTIME DURATION		FLIGHT CENTER STAMP	
TODAY			☐ INSTRUCTOR
TO DATE			☐ FLIGHT TUTOR
ALL TIME			☐ FLIGHT BUDDY

SIGNATURE

_____

LOCATION		DATE
PARAGLIDER		
PARAMOTOR		/ /

LAUNCH TYPE		AIRTIME	
		AIR DISTANCE	

WEATHER CONDITION	☀ ☁ ❄ ⚡ 🌬	TIME OF YEAR	🌷 ☀ 🍃 ❄

FLIGHT START	🕐	GEAR CHECKLIST	
FLIGHT FINISH		☐ PARAGLIDER	☐ HARNESS
SLOPE GRADIENT	↑ ↓	☐ GOGGLES	☐ HELMET
		☐ RESERVE	☐ GLOVES

LAUNCH LOCATION	LANDING LOCATION

NOTES & OBSERVATIONS

_____

_____

_____

AIRTIME DURATION		FLIGHT CENTER STAMP	
TODAY			☐ INSTRUCTOR
TO DATE			☐ FLIGHT TUTOR
ALL TIME			☐ FLIGHT BUDDY

SIGNATURE _____

LOCATION		DATE
PARAGLIDER		
PARAMOTOR		/ /

LAUNCH TYPE		AIRTIME	
		AIR DISTANCE	

WEATHER CONDITION	☀ ☁ ❄ ⛆ 🌬	TIME OF YEAR	🌷 ☀ 🍃 ❄

FLIGHT START	🕐	GEAR CHECKLIST	
FLIGHT FINISH		☐ PARAGLIDER	☐ HARNESS
SLOPE GRADIENT	↑ ↓	☐ GOGGLES	☐ HELMET
		☐ RESERVE	☐ GLOVES

LAUNCH LOCATION	LANDING LOCATION

NOTES & OBSERVATIONS

_____

_____

_____

AIRTIME DURATION		FLIGHT CENTER STAMP	
TODAY			☐ INSTRUCTOR
TO DATE			☐ FLIGHT TUTOR
ALL TIME			☐ FLIGHT BUDDY

SIGNATURE

_____

LOCATION		DATE
PARAGLIDER		
PARAMOTOR		/ /

LAUNCH TYPE		AIRTIME	
		AIR DISTANCE	

WEATHER CONDITION	☀ ☁ ❄ ⛈ 🌬	TIME OF YEAR	🌷 ☀ 🍁 ❄

FLIGHT START	🕐	GEAR CHECKLIST	
FLIGHT FINISH		☐ PARAGLIDER	☐ HARNESS
SLOPE GRADIENT	↑ ↓	☐ GOGGLES	☐ HELMET
		☐ RESERVE	☐ GLOVES

LAUNCH LOCATION	LANDING LOCATION

NOTES & OBSERVATIONS

_____

_____

_____

AIRTIME DURATION		FLIGHT CENTER STAMP	
TODAY			☐ INSTRUCTOR
TO DATE			☐ FLIGHT TUTOR
ALL TIME			☐ FLIGHT BUDDY

SIGNATURE

_____

LOCATION		DATE
PARAGLIDER		
PARAMOTOR		/ /

LAUNCH TYPE		AIRTIME	
		AIR DISTANCE	

WEATHER CONDITION	☀ ☁ ❄ ⛈ 🌬	TIME OF YEAR	🌷 ☀ 🍁 ❄

FLIGHT START	🕐		GEAR CHECKLIST	
FLIGHT FINISH			☐ PARAGLIDER	☐ HARNESS
SLOPE GRADIENT	↑ ↓		☐ GOGGLES	☐ HELMET
			☐ RESERVE	☐ GLOVES

LAUNCH LOCATION | LANDING LOCATION

NOTES & OBSERVATIONS

_____

_____

_____

AIRTIME DURATION

TODAY	
TO DATE	
ALL TIME	

FLIGHT CENTER STAMP

☐ INSTRUCTOR

☐ FLIGHT TUTOR

☐ FLIGHT BUDDY

SIGNATURE

_____

LOCATION		DATE
PARAGLIDER		
PARAMOTOR		/ /

LAUNCH TYPE		AIRTIME	
		AIR DISTANCE	

WEATHER CONDITION	☀ ☁ ❄ ⛈ 🌬	TIME OF YEAR	🌷 ☀ 🍃 ❄

FLIGHT START	🕐	GEAR CHECKLIST	
FLIGHT FINISH		☐ PARAGLIDER	☐ HARNESS
SLOPE GRADIENT	↑↓	☐ GOGGLES	☐ HELMET
		☐ RESERVE	☐ GLOVES

LAUNCH LOCATION	LANDING LOCATION

NOTES & OBSERVATIONS

_____

_____

_____

AIRTIME DURATION		FLIGHT CENTER STAMP	
TODAY			☐ INSTRUCTOR
TO DATE			☐ FLIGHT TUTOR
ALL TIME			☐ FLIGHT BUDDY

SIGNATURE _____

LOCATION		DATE
PARAGLIDER		
PARAMOTOR		/ /

LAUNCH TYPE		AIRTIME	
		AIR DISTANCE	

WEATHER CONDITION	☀ ☁ ❄ ⛈ 🌬	TIME OF YEAR	🌷 ☀ 🍂 ❄

FLIGHT START	🕐	GEAR CHECKLIST	
FLIGHT FINISH		☐ PARAGLIDER	☐ HARNESS
SLOPE GRADIENT	↑ ↓	☐ GOGGLES	☐ HELMET
		☐ RESERVE	☐ GLOVES

LAUNCH LOCATION	LANDING LOCATION

NOTES & OBSERVATIONS

AIRTIME DURATION		FLIGHT CENTER STAMP	
TODAY			☐ INSTRUCTOR
TO DATE			☐ FLIGHT TUTOR
ALL TIME			☐ FLIGHT BUDDY

SIGNATURE

LOCATION		DATE
PARAGLIDER		
PARAMOTOR		/ /

LAUNCH TYPE		AIRTIME	
		AIR DISTANCE	

WEATHER CONDITION	☀ ☁ ❄ ⚡ 🌬	TIME OF YEAR	🌷 ☀ 🍃 ❄

FLIGHT START	🕐	GEAR CHECKLIST	
FLIGHT FINISH		☐ PARAGLIDER	☐ HARNESS
SLOPE GRADIENT	↑ ↓	☐ GOGGLES	☐ HELMET
		☐ RESERVE	☐ GLOVES

LAUNCH LOCATION	LANDING LOCATION

NOTES & OBSERVATIONS

_____

_____

_____

AIRTIME DURATION		FLIGHT CENTER STAMP	
TODAY			☐ INSTRUCTOR
TO DATE			☐ FLIGHT TUTOR
ALL TIME			☐ FLIGHT BUDDY

SIGNATURE _____

LOCATION		DATE
PARAGLIDER		
PARAMOTOR		/ /

LAUNCH TYPE		AIRTIME	
		AIR DISTANCE	

WEATHER CONDITION	☀ ☁ ❄ ⛈ 〰	TIME OF YEAR	🌷 ☀ 🍂 ❄

FLIGHT START	🕐	GEAR CHECKLIST	
FLIGHT FINISH		☐ PARAGLIDER	☐ HARNESS
SLOPE GRADIENT	↑↓	☐ GOGGLES	☐ HELMET
		☐ RESERVE	☐ GLOVES

LAUNCH LOCATION	LANDING LOCATION

NOTES & OBSERVATIONS

_____

_____

_____

AIRTIME DURATION		FLIGHT CENTER STAMP	
TODAY			☐ INSTRUCTOR
TO DATE			☐ FLIGHT TUTOR
ALL TIME			☐ FLIGHT BUDDY

SIGNATURE

_____

LOCATION		DATE
PARAGLIDER		
PARAMOTOR		/ /

LAUNCH TYPE		AIRTIME	
		AIR DISTANCE	

WEATHER CONDITION	☀ ☁ ❄ ⛈ 🌬	TIME OF YEAR	🌷 ☀ 🍃 ❄

FLIGHT START	🕐	GEAR CHECKLIST	
FLIGHT FINISH		☐ PARAGLIDER	☐ HARNESS
SLOPE GRADIENT	↑↓	☐ GOGGLES	☐ HELMET
		☐ RESERVE	☐ GLOVES

LAUNCH LOCATION	LANDING LOCATION

NOTES & OBSERVATIONS

AIRTIME DURATION		FLIGHT CENTER STAMP	
TODAY			☐ INSTRUCTOR
TO DATE			☐ FLIGHT TUTOR
ALL TIME			☐ FLIGHT BUDDY

SIGNATURE

LOCATION		DATE	
PARAGLIDER			
PARAMOTOR		/ /	

LAUNCH TYPE		AIRTIME	
		AIR DISTANCE	

WEATHER CONDITION	☀ ☁ ❄ ⛈ 🌬	TIME OF YEAR	🌷 ☀ 🍁 ❄

FLIGHT START	🕐	GEAR CHECKLIST	
FLIGHT FINISH		☐ PARAGLIDER	☐ HARNESS
SLOPE GRADIENT	↑ ↓	☐ GOGGLES	☐ HELMET
		☐ RESERVE	☐ GLOVES

LAUNCH LOCATION | LANDING LOCATION

NOTES & OBSERVATIONS

_____

_____

_____

AIRTIME DURATION

TODAY	
TO DATE	
ALL TIME	

FLIGHT CENTER STAMP

☐ INSTRUCTOR

☐ FLIGHT TUTOR

☐ FLIGHT BUDDY

SIGNATURE

_____

LOCATION		DATE
PARAGLIDER		
PARAMOTOR		/ /

LAUNCH TYPE		AIRTIME	
		AIR DISTANCE	

WEATHER CONDITION	☀ ☁ ❄ ⚡ 💨	TIME OF YEAR	🌷 ☀ 🍂 ❄

FLIGHT START	🕐	GEAR CHECKLIST	
FLIGHT FINISH		☐ PARAGLIDER	☐ HARNESS
SLOPE GRADIENT	↑↓	☐ GOGGLES	☐ HELMET
		☐ RESERVE	☐ GLOVES

LAUNCH LOCATION	LANDING LOCATION

NOTES & OBSERVATIONS

_____

_____

_____

AIRTIME DURATION		FLIGHT CENTER STAMP
TODAY		☐ INSTRUCTOR
TO DATE		☐ FLIGHT TUTOR
ALL TIME		☐ FLIGHT BUDDY

SIGNATURE

_____

LOCATION		DATE	
PARAGLIDER			
PARAMOTOR		/ /	

LAUNCH TYPE		AIRTIME	
		AIR DISTANCE	

WEATHER CONDITION	☀ ☁ ❄ ⛈ 🌬	TIME OF YEAR	🌷 ☀ 🍁 ❄

FLIGHT START	🕐	GEAR CHECKLIST	
FLIGHT FINISH		☐ PARAGLIDER	☐ HARNESS
SLOPE GRADIENT	↑ ↓	☐ GOGGLES	☐ HELMET
		☐ RESERVE	☐ GLOVES

LAUNCH LOCATION	LANDING LOCATION

NOTES & OBSERVATIONS

_____

_____

AIRTIME DURATION		FLIGHT CENTER STAMP	
TODAY			☐ INSTRUCTOR
TO DATE			☐ FLIGHT TUTOR
ALL TIME			☐ FLIGHT BUDDY

SIGNATURE

_____

LOCATION		DATE
PARAGLIDER		
PARAMOTOR		/ /

LAUNCH TYPE		AIRTIME	
		AIR DISTANCE	

WEATHER CONDITION	☀ ☁ ❄ ⚡ 💨	TIME OF YEAR	🌷 ☀ 🍃 ❄

FLIGHT START	🕐	GEAR CHECKLIST	
FLIGHT FINISH		☐ PARAGLIDER	☐ HARNESS
SLOPE GRADIENT	↑ ↓	☐ GOGGLES	☐ HELMET
		☐ RESERVE	☐ GLOVES

LAUNCH LOCATION	LANDING LOCATION

NOTES & OBSERVATIONS

AIRTIME DURATION		FLIGHT CENTER STAMP	
TODAY			☐ INSTRUCTOR
TO DATE			☐ FLIGHT TUTOR
ALL TIME			☐ FLIGHT BUDDY

SIGNATURE

LOCATION		DATE
PARAGLIDER		
PARAMOTOR		/ /

LAUNCH TYPE		AIRTIME	
		AIR DISTANCE	

WEATHER CONDITION	☀ ☔ ❄ ⛈ 🌬	TIME OF YEAR	🌷 ☀ 🍃 ❄

FLIGHT START	🕐	GEAR CHECKLIST	
FLIGHT FINISH		☐ PARAGLIDER	☐ HARNESS
SLOPE GRADIENT	↑ ↓	☐ GOGGLES	☐ HELMET
		☐ RESERVE	☐ GLOVES

LAUNCH LOCATION	LANDING LOCATION

NOTES & OBSERVATIONS

_____

_____

_____

AIRTIME DURATION		FLIGHT CENTER STAMP	
TODAY			☐ INSTRUCTOR
TO DATE			☐ FLIGHT TUTOR
ALL TIME			☐ FLIGHT BUDDY

SIGNATURE

_____

LOCATION		DATE
PARAGLIDER		
PARAMOTOR		/ /

LAUNCH TYPE		AIRTIME	
		AIR DISTANCE	

WEATHER CONDITION	☀ ☁ ❄ ⛈ 🌬	TIME OF YEAR	🌷 ☀ 🍃 ❄

FLIGHT START	🕐	GEAR CHECKLIST	
FLIGHT FINISH		☐ PARAGLIDER	☐ HARNESS
SLOPE GRADIENT	↑ ↓	☐ GOGGLES	☐ HELMET
		☐ RESERVE	☐ GLOVES

LAUNCH LOCATION	LANDING LOCATION

NOTES & OBSERVATIONS

_____

_____

_____

AIRTIME DURATION		FLIGHT CENTER STAMP	
TODAY			☐ INSTRUCTOR
TO DATE			☐ FLIGHT TUTOR
ALL TIME			☐ FLIGHT BUDDY

SIGNATURE

_____

LOCATION		DATE
PARAGLIDER		
PARAMOTOR		/ /

LAUNCH TYPE		AIRTIME	
		AIR DISTANCE	

WEATHER CONDITION	☀ ☔ ❄ ⛈ 🌬	TIME OF YEAR	🌷 ☀ 🍂 ❄

FLIGHT START	🕐	GEAR CHECKLIST	
FLIGHT FINISH		☐ PARAGLIDER	☐ HARNESS
SLOPE GRADIENT	↑ ↓	☐ GOGGLES	☐ HELMET
		☐ RESERVE	☐ GLOVES

LAUNCH LOCATION	LANDING LOCATION

NOTES & OBSERVATIONS

_____

_____

_____

AIRTIME DURATION		FLIGHT CENTER STAMP	
TODAY			☐ INSTRUCTOR
TO DATE			☐ FLIGHT TUTOR
ALL TIME			☐ FLIGHT BUDDY

SIGNATURE

_____

LOCATION		DATE
PARAGLIDER		
PARAMOTOR		/ /

LAUNCH TYPE		AIRTIME	
		AIR DISTANCE	

WEATHER CONDITION	☀ ☁ ❄ ⛈ 💨	TIME OF YEAR	🌷 ☀ 🍃 ❄

FLIGHT START	🕐	GEAR CHECKLIST	
FLIGHT FINISH		☐ PARAGLIDER	☐ HARNESS
SLOPE GRADIENT	↑↓	☐ GOGGLES	☐ HELMET
		☐ RESERVE	☐ GLOVES

LAUNCH LOCATION

LANDING LOCATION

NOTES & OBSERVATIONS

_____

_____

_____

AIRTIME DURATION

TODAY	
TO DATE	
ALL TIME	

FLIGHT CENTER STAMP

☐ INSTRUCTOR

☐ FLIGHT TUTOR

☐ FLIGHT BUDDY

SIGNATURE

_____

LOCATION		DATE	
PARAGLIDER			
PARAMOTOR		/ /	

LAUNCH TYPE		AIRTIME	
		AIR DISTANCE	

WEATHER CONDITION	☀ ☁ ❄ ⛈ 💨	TIME OF YEAR	🌷 ☀ 🍂 ❄

FLIGHT START	🕐	GEAR CHECKLIST	
FLIGHT FINISH		☐ PARAGLIDER	☐ HARNESS
SLOPE GRADIENT	↑ ↓	☐ GOGGLES	☐ HELMET
		☐ RESERVE	☐ GLOVES

LAUNCH LOCATION	LANDING LOCATION

NOTES & OBSERVATIONS

_____

_____

_____

AIRTIME DURATION		FLIGHT CENTER STAMP	
TODAY			☐ INSTRUCTOR
TO DATE			☐ FLIGHT TUTOR
ALL TIME			☐ FLIGHT BUDDY

SIGNATURE

_____

LOCATION		DATE
PARAGLIDER		
PARAMOTOR		/ /

LAUNCH TYPE		AIRTIME	
		AIR DISTANCE	

WEATHER CONDITION	☀ ☁ ❄ ⛈ 🌬	TIME OF YEAR	🌷 ☀ 🍃 ❄

FLIGHT START	🕐	GEAR CHECKLIST	
FLIGHT FINISH		☐ PARAGLIDER	☐ HARNESS
SLOPE GRADIENT	↑↓	☐ GOGGLES	☐ HELMET
		☐ RESERVE	☐ GLOVES

LAUNCH LOCATION	LANDING LOCATION

NOTES & OBSERVATIONS

AIRTIME DURATION		FLIGHT CENTER STAMP	
TODAY			☐ INSTRUCTOR
TO DATE			☐ FLIGHT TUTOR
ALL TIME			☐ FLIGHT BUDDY

SIGNATURE

LOCATION		DATE
PARAGLIDER		
PARAMOTOR		/ /

LAUNCH TYPE		AIRTIME	
		AIR DISTANCE	

WEATHER CONDITION	☀ ☁ ❄ ⛈ 🌬	TIME OF YEAR	🌷 ☀ 🍃 ❄

FLIGHT START	🕐	GEAR CHECKLIST	
FLIGHT FINISH		☐ PARAGLIDER	☐ HARNESS
SLOPE GRADIENT	↑↓	☐ GOGGLES	☐ HELMET
		☐ RESERVE	☐ GLOVES

LAUNCH LOCATION	LANDING LOCATION

NOTES & OBSERVATIONS

_____

_____

_____

AIRTIME DURATION

		FLIGHT CENTER STAMP	
TODAY			☐ INSTRUCTOR
TO DATE			☐ FLIGHT TUTOR
ALL TIME			☐ FLIGHT BUDDY

SIGNATURE

_____

Thanks For Reading!

Just a quick message to thank you so much for picking up one of our books! Our sincere hope is that this book has given you the value we always look to provide, and hope we can continue to produce quality books that will in anyway contribute to a better quality of life for our readers.

We are a small independent publisher based in London, UK and we work with talented authors from around the world, who dedicate every ounce of their effort to craft these memorable books for your reading pleasure.

The author of this title would love to hear about your experience with the book, and your review will go a long way to provide them with the insight and encouragement they need to keep creating the kind of books you want to read.

Your Opinion Makes a Real Difference.

If you want to let us know what you thought about the book, please visit the Amazon website and give us your review. We read every single review, no matter how long or short!

Thanks again and until the next time....

HAPPY READING!

Made in United States
Troutdale, OR
12/15/2024

26452264R00070